First and Last

A Devotional for Hestia

Edited by Terence P. Ward

Copyright © 2017 by Neos Alexandria/Bibliotheca Alexandrina Incorporated

All rights reserved. No part of this book may be reproduced by any means or in any form whatsoever without written permission from the author(s), except for brief quotations embodied in literary articles or reviews. Copyright reverts to original authors after publication.

Cover font: the Fell Types are digitally reproduced by Igino Marini. www.iginomarini.com

Prytaneum
by Devon Power

Dedication

To the eldest and the youngest
the least and the greatest
the quiet center of creation

Table of Contents

Prytaneum
    by Devon Power ... 3

Dedication ... 4
Introduction
    by Terentios Poseidonides
    (Terence P. Ward) ... 10
From the Desk of the Editor-in-Chief
    by Rebecca Buchanan ... 12

First and Last
    by Jennifer Lawrence ... 13
Musings on Hestia
    by Merit Brokaw ... 15
An Offering to Hestia
    by Alexeigynaix ... 21
Hymn to Hestia VI
    by Rebecca Buchanan ... 22
For Hestia, on the roads
    by Terentios Poseidonides ... 23
A Ritual for Hestia: Home Blessing
    by Amanda Artemisia Forrester ... 24
Wanderer's Hymn
    by Allie Hayes ... 28
Invocation to Hestia
    by Jay Logan ... 29

A Call to Hestia
>   by Tina Georgitsis ... 31
Ἑστία ἐστι
>   by Edward P. Butler ... 33
Hearth and Fire
>   by Chelsea Luellon Bolton ... 47
The Tale of Erinna and Philôn
>   by Rebecca Buchanan ... 51

Invocation
>   *by Frederic Lord Leighton* ... 58

The First of February
>   by Eric Paul Shaffer ... 59
Hestia's Tale
>   by Merit Brokaw ... 61
Forever My Own
>   by Gerri Leen ... 84
Queen of Hearth and Home I
>   by Kathy Mac ... 86
The Sacred Fire
>   by David W. Landrum ... 87
The Bath of Hestia
>   by P. Sufenas Virius Lupus ... 100
Guess Who's Coming to Dinner:
>   Hestia, Hospitality, and Interstate Relations in Classical Athens
>   by Nicholas D. Cross ... 102
Hestia of the Campfire
>   by Lyssa Little Bear ... 118

Prayer for a Peaceful Home
>	by Amanda Artemisia Forrester ... 119
Gluten-Free Italian Spaghetti Meatballs
>	by Alexeigynaix ... 120
To Hestia on Her Birth-Feast
>	by P. Sufenas Virius Lupus ... 123

Hymn to Hestia
>	*by Jessica Orlando and Peter Ringo ... 124*

Queen of Hearth and Home II
>	by Kathy Mac ... 128
Salmon Dorie Recipe: An Offering for Hestia
>	by Sparrow ... 129
Hestia's Domestic Bliss
>	by Verónica Pamoukaghlián ... 131
An Unusual Holiday for Hestia in Roman Egypt
>	by P. Sufenas Virius Lupus ... 133
Hestia's Colors
>	by Rachel Iriswings ... 142
To Hestia
>	by Karen Salvati Harper ... 144
Hestia, First and Last
>	by Amanda Artemisia Forrester ... 146
Hymn to Hestia
>	by Leni Hester ... 148
In Praise of Hestia
>	by Lyssa Little Bear ... 149
Hearthsong
>	by Jason Ross Inczauskis ... 150

Darkness Bright
>	by Jay Logan ... 152
Goddess of Little Renown, But Lasting Prominence
>	by Elani Temperance ... 154
Hestia of the Flame
>	by Amanda Artemisia Forrester ... 169

Hestia ... 171

A Tale of Vanity and Modesty: My Covering Story
>	by Lyssa Little Bear ... 172
Prayer to Hestia
>	by Merit Brokaw ... 176
The Hearth as Witness
>	by Gerri Leen ... 178
Hestia, The Heart of the Cosmic Order
>	by Ann Hatzakis ... 180
Hymn to the Fire of Naukratis
>	by P. Sufenas Virius Lupus ... 184
Haikus for Hestia
>	by Rebecca Buchanan ... 187
Hestia: An Acrostic
>	by T.J. O'Hare ... 188
O Keeper of the Flame
>	by Lyssa Little Bear ... 189
In Honour of Hestia
>	by Ariadni Rainbird ... 190
To Hestia
>	by Jessi Robinson ... 191

Prayer to Hestia, To Be Spoken By the Dying
    by Alexeigynaix … 192
The First and the Last
    by Sparrow … 193

Hestia
    by Laurie Goodhart … 195

Appendix A: Epithets of Hestia
    compiled by Chelsea Luellon Bolton … 196
Appendix B: Public Domain Hymns
    to Hestia … 198
Appendix C: Our Contributors … 200
Appendix D: About Bibliotheca Alexandrina — Current Titles — Forthcoming Titles … 213

Introduction

While Hestia may not be one of the better-known goddesses, in some sense she really needs no introduction. In many — perhaps even most — modern Hellenic traditions she is the first to be given offerings, and the same held true in antiquity. That position of respect is reflected in the myth of her birth: first child of Kronos and Rhea, she was also the first to be devoured by her father; when Zeus freed his siblings, Hestia was thus the last disgorged. First and last born, Hestia accepts all offerings, and is due a portion both first and last. That role in receiving offerings is in turn reflected in Hestia's connection to the hearth, for sacrifices are traditionally burned: she is the central fire which warms and lights all homes, enabling cooking and all manner of vital domestic activity on the mortal plane, in Olympos, and some believe even in the underworld.

At the same time, little more is known of Hestia. Being the primary goddess of the domestic sphere didn't inspire many Hellenes to write hymns describing her attributes and the practices used to honor her. We know from surviving myths that she was wooed by Apollon and Poseidon, but preferred to stay unmarried. Another story tells of a sexual assault by Priapus, narrowly averted. That link of information perhaps helped Graves conclude that she abdicated her Olympian throne, but that story is not entirely accepted by her followers today. There are other new tales within this volume, and through them the reader might imagine how gaps in this quiet goddess' character and exploits could be filled.

That is what this book is, primarily: a way for 21st-century Hellenic Polytheists to fill in gaps of belief, practice, and understanding which were not handed down through the intervening millennia. Several writers herein opted to expound upon the existing scholarship; these essays, then, form the foundation of the work and begin its several informal sections. Within these can be found tales that are perhaps more palatable than Graves', as well as actual recipes, and other devotional work for this virgin goddess. Throughout all are interwoven poetry and hymns, the authors of two of which even provided sheet music.

What the contents of *First and Last* demonstrate without doubt is that Hestia remains highly revered and respected. As in ancient days, she receives both the least and greatest of offerings. May she never be forgotten.

Terentios Poseidonides
(Terence P. Ward)

From the Desk of the Editor-in-Chief

Hestia is one of the great unknowns in Hellenic polytheism; or, perhaps, one of the lesser-knowns is a better way of putting it. She was so central to ancient beliefs and practices that the Greeks actually wrote down very little about Her. She simply Was.

And Is.

And so we find ourselves having to recreate Her worship, craft new devotional practices, write new hymns and songs and even myths.

It is a worthy endeavor, and one that has only just begun.

Rebecca Buchanan
Winter 2017

First and Last

by Jennifer Lawrence

To you, the first and the last, fair lady;
the hearth of the home,
the flame in the hearth,
the food cooking in the flame;
these things are yours,
quiet and patient, clean and calm,
and generous, always,
giving of your hospitality
to all who come to your door,
accepting them into your home,
breaking bread with them,
seeing they are clad in garb
clean and without tear,
and giving them the best of beds
and best of pillows
on which to lay their heads at night.
You turn aside no welcome guest,
frowning only on the rude, the disrespectful,
those burdened with hubris and miasma.
And so great is your giving heart
that, when Zeus' son by Semele
came to the halls of Mount Olympus,
rather than bear a fight breaking out
among those deathless ones, to see
Dionysus seated there as was his due,
you willingly gave up your seat to him,

preventing loud voices raised in discord,
and claimed only the central fire to tend,
and once again sharing the best that you had
with the newly-come guest
so that he, too, might feel welcome.
Hestia, home and hearth, fire and food,
all that is welcome in the *oikos*:
never shall I let your flame die out.

Musings on Hestia
by Merit Brokaw

This is a goddess who often seems to get left out or receives only the token first and last offerings. A rather quiet-seeming divinity, not as flashy mythologically as the other Greek divinities and often taken for granted, I think. She is one of my favorite divinities, however, and always has been. One of the occurrences that triggered my musings was a comment made about hot flashes:

"You know the sudden flash of heat you get when you open the door on a hot oven? That is what a hot flash is like, except it is coming from inside."

A pretty accurate description of what menopausal women deal with multiple times a day. This led me to ponder Hestia's place in a woman's life. While the gods are more than archetypes, they also can fulfill that function. Of all the "major" Greek divinities, Hestia is the only one who doesn't have an obvious place in a woman's cycle, from child to elder; or does she? Artemis is seen as the young child running free. Athene, I see as the transition to young adult. Aphrodite is sexual awakening. Persephone is the transition from young adult to woman and wife. Hera is the wife. Demeter is the mother.

But what about Hestia, lady of flame? She belongs to all and yet to none. Her flame is about home, but also about transformation. Maybe she is the menopause transformation. The heat of transformation, belongs to all (family, job, parents, etc.), but yet the hormonal change also forces you to look to yourself more and again.

Hestia is looked upon as the eldest and the youngest of the Olympian siblings (as opposed to the Olympian children like Athene and Hermes). She is the first born to Rhea, but the last disgorged by Kronos. She is the most retiring of the six siblings in that she doesn't like conflict, but do not think that she is harmless; fire can burn just as easily as it can warm. As the first born and first consumed, she was alone and then got to watch as each of her siblings joined her in that paternal prison. I believe that she raised her siblings as well as she could with the limited knowledge and resources that she had. As the eldest in my own small family, I can see how she tried to guide, care for, and shape her younger siblings, and how that shaped her personality when she was "reborn." She is very much the maternal female who has never given birth. Her concern has always been focused on the wellbeing of the individual, the family unit, and with providing the care needed so that growth can happen. She is the behind-the-scenes caretaker who is often taken for granted and forgotten, only remembered if she isn't there or things don't go smoothly.

That isn't to say she isn't loved by her siblings, because she is. For four of them, she is the only mother figure they've ever known. Yet they were happy to leave her realm of control and seem to rather look at her as backward, slow, out of touch, unimportant ... until there is a problem. Then they return to her hearth to talk about the issues, the changes in their lives. Even if she doesn't say a word, her mere presence, her attitude of listening, helps them gain perspective so that decisions can be made. I see her as a colorful, laughter-loving divinity full of surprises in the same way that a kitchen, which is always the center of any party no matter how a hostess tries for otherwise, is full of wonderful and surprising things.

One of the things I used to do before I had a child was to brew up a couple cups of tea, place one on the altar before her candle (which I do not leave burning all the time, but light before each ritual and you know what, I think she is perfectly fine with that, the practical goddess that she is) and talk with her about all the things happening in my life. It was nice to have a listener that didn't judge, who was happy to listen and just be there. Someone I didn't have to worry about how what I was saying may affect them or change the way they think of me. It was an excellent way to clear my head during stressful times. I really need to go back to doing that.

Whenever there was a change in the household, the change was brought to the hearth to tell the goddess ... whether a birth, a death, et cetera. Fire is an element of transition and menopause is essentially the body transitioning from a reproductive to an unproductive state. In my own experience it effects every function in my body, from mental outlook to sleep cycles to weight to digestion. It is a natural function of the body that transitions the woman from the physical "mother" status to the physical "crone" status. It is every bit as much a mental process as it is a physical process. I'm having to face the fact that I will never again be that young, slim, sexy lady again and in a society that seems to prize that above all, it is very stressful transition. Stress makes hot flashes happen more often, and more intensely.

Appropriately, the only plant that I found as even tentatively associated with Hestia is the chaste tree. From my research, it appears the chasteberry is an adaptogen that helps the female system to normalize. Its uses include dealing with PMS, irregular periods, and alleviating menopause symptoms. It is something I plan to try as another weapon in my arsenal to get me through the physical transition that often seems like cruel and unusual torture when I can't sleep more than three to four hours a night.

I also discovered that one of Hestia's symbols is the kettle. The oldest kettle found comes from Mesopotamia way before the common era and looks very similar to the tea kettles still in use today. They were used to boil water to make it safe for drinking. I find this association ironic, because I collect tea pots. To me they are a symbol of hospitality and friendship; a symbol of warmth and friendly conversation. Out of curiosity, I looked up the etymology of the word *kettle* and on the same page is the similar etymology of *cauldron*.

kettle (n.) Old English cetil (Mercian), from Proto-Germanic *katilaz (compare Old Saxon ketel, Old Frisian zetel, Middle Dutch ketel, Old High German kezzil, German Kessel), probably from Latin catillus "deep pan or dish for cooking," diminutive of catinus "bowl, dish, pot." One of the few Latin loan-words in Proto-Germanic ... Spelling with a -k- (c.1300) probably is from influence of Old Norse cognate ketill. The smaller sense of "tea-kettle" is attested by 1769.

cauldron (n.) c.1300 caudron, from Anglo-French caudrun, Old North French cauderon (Old French chauderon "cauldron, kettle"), from augmentative of Late Latin caldaria "cooking pot" (source of Spanish calderon, Italian calderone), from Latin calidarium "hot bath," from calidus "warm, hot" The -l- was inserted 15c. in imitation of Latin.

Every time I see a bowl or cauldron with a female divinity, I'm going to think of Hestia. It also adds some interesting ideas for altar decorations since representations of Ceridwen are easier to find than representations of Hestia (which typically fall short in my opinion, however artistically lovely they are). I am amused that the three bowls I painted and added to my main altar also unintentionally honored her.

Other items of interest:
· Hestia is also the divinity of home building
· she presides over cooking and hospitality
· as goddess of the sacrificial flame, she shares in every burnt sacrifice and in the communal feast that follows after such sacrifices
· she received oaths spoken at the hearth
· the hearth was also the place to seek asylum
· "true" fires are lit by friction (which makes lighters and matches perfectly acceptable ways of lighting her fires) or by magnifying glass
· often conflated with: Kybele, Gaia, Demeter, Persephone, and Artemis
· typical sacrifices: fruit, water, oil, sweet wine, and one-year-old cows

An Offering to Hestia

by Alexeigynaix

The past day's dishes languish
in my sink, unwashed.
This should not be:
the home disheveled,
unkempt.
I take up the sponge
and scrubbie,
a drop of dish soap,
and say,
"Hestia, you who guard
the hearth and home,
I offer this time to you."
The dishes sparkle
in the sun.

Hymn to Hestía VI
by Rebecca Buchanan

she is the ancient flame:
eldest
and
youngest
child of earth

For Hestia, on the roads

by Terentios Poseidonides

Hestia, if I have ever poured
libations in your name,
hear this humble offering:
your praises I proclaim.
You are my heart, my rock, my source;
where I find you is my home.
Though wander roads aplenty I
you are my hearth, my fire; home.
To bring my fire, rekindle your hearth
to offer first and last, as told
I honor she who blesses my home
and keeps me close upon the road.

A Ritual for Hestia:
Home Blessing

by Amanda Artemisia Forrester

A ritual for Hestia should be made when the house is clean. This may sound silly, but it's true. Whenever I pray to or do ritual for Hestia, I get an irresistible urge to clean. Every six months or so I do a full cleaning of the entire house, and re-bless my home. As the only Pagan in my household I observe this ritual alone, but if at all possible, it should be done with other family members. Hestia is the Goddess who guards not only the home, but family relationships.

This ritual should be performed at the altar to the household Gods. If you don't have one, then set up on the stove, the modern day hearth.

You will need :

• a tall candle, either white, the color of purity, or orange or red, the colors of fire
• khernips (lustral water)
• grain such as barley or wheat
• honey
• small change or a few dollar bills, and
• an offering plate.

After cleaning the house, make sure you are wearing clean clothes. If your attire was dirtied while cleaning, than take the time to change. Your outfit doesn't have to be fancy, as Hestia is a simple Goddess and simple clothes will do; just be sure you are clean.

When you are ready to begin, approach the altar. After washing your hands and face in the khernips, light the hearth candle. This candle will be the symbol of Hestia, the eternal flame. Remember that Hestia dwells within the flame, and treat it accordingly. Raise your hands to the sky, and staring into the flame, say:

Holy Hestia, who burns at the center of Olympos, the center of the city, and the center of the home, I call you to enter my house. Make these four walls, this roof and floor, into a home. Purify my dwelling place, and bring your peace and light to me and mine. May all who dwell within this home be filled with your radiance, gentle Goddess.

Read either the Homeric or the Orphic hymn to Hestia:

Homeric Hymn 24 (To Hestia)
Hestia, in the high dwellings of all,
both deathless Gods and men who walk on earth,
you have gained an everlasting abode and highest
      honor:
glorious is your portion and your right.
For without you mortals hold no banquet, –
where one does not duly pour sweet wine

in offering to Hestia both first and last.
And you, Argeiphontes [Hermes], son of Zeus and
> Maia,
. . . be favorable and help us, you and Hestia,
the worshipful and dear.
Come and dwell in this glorious house in friendship
> together;
for you two, well knowing the noble actions of men,
aid on their wisdom and their strength.
Hail, Daughter of Kronos, and you also, Hermes.

Orphic Hymn 84 (To Hestia)
Daughter of Kronos, venerable dame,
who dwellest amidst great fire's eternal flame;
in sacred rites these ministers are thine,
mystics much blessed, holy and divine.
In thee the Gods have fixed their dwelling place,
strong,stable basis of the mortal race.
Eternal, much formed, ever florid queen,
laughing and blessed, and of lovely mien;
accept these rites, accord each just desire,
and gentle health and needful good inspire.

Read the following prayer, and present Hestia with each of the offerings named by placing it on the offering plate.

Mild Goddess, I bring you grain, that our pantry will be filled and those who dwell within this home continue to be fed. Beauteous Hestia, I offer you honey, that I and my family be filled with your sweetness and charity. Lastly, I offer you these coins, that our household continue to prosper.

Stand before the altar or the hearth for a moment, hands facing the sky, and meditate in silence on the presence of the Goddess. Leave the offerings on the offering plate for a few hours. Later, bury all the offerings outside. Allow the candle to keep burning until you go to bed. If you are able to do so safely, have a candle on the altar to the household Gods burning whenever you are at home and awake, only blowing it out when you leave the house or go to sleep.

Wanderer's Hymn

by Allie Hayes

Although I may run with deer-shooting Artemis
in the mountain forests,
Although I may sing to beautiful Aphrodite
on the foam covered sea shore,
Although I may seek the mysteries
of night-wandering Hekate at the crossroads,
Although I may pour libations
to lovely crowned Demeter
in golden fields of grain,
It is always you, Hestia, that I return to.

You are the gentle flame
that gives warmth to the weary,
You soothe away troubles
with the comfort of the hearth,
You are the stable foundation
that always welcomes my return.

And even when I travel along dusty roads,
One thousand miles away from home,
You are still with me,
Burning brightly,
In my heart.

Invocation to Hestia

by Jay Logan

Hail to Hestia, goddess of the eternal flame
Hail to you great lady, who is the center of all things
The foundation upon which we build
The axis around which we turn

Hail to you, first among the gods, yet last
The alpha and omega
The beginning and end of all things.

Hail to you, who is the heart of my heart
The heart of this hearth and home
The heart of every city and town
The heart of every temple and altar
The heart of Mount Olympos
And the heart of sacred Delphi, the navel of the
      world.

Hail to you who is the heart of the living earth
And the heart of the radiant sun
Around which the worlds turn
Hail to you great lady, who sits on the throne of
      Polaris
Encircled by the mighty Dragon
Around which the very wheel of the cosmos turns.

Hail to you great lady
Hail to you, on this day and all days.

Khaire Hestia!

A Call to Hestia

by Tina Georgitsis

I call to you through hidden tome
Headmistress of the hearth and home
I call to you through hidden tome

Hair shrouded with a veil
Offerings of khernips from the pail
Hair shrouded with a veil

Resins lit along with the sacred flame
So bright and in your name
Resins lit along with the sacred flame

Chanting petitions of renewal and purification
Messenger of state, architect of completion
Chanting petitions of renewal and purification

Chalice raised filled with sweet wine
Pour a sacrifice straight off the vine
Chalice raised filled with sweet wine

I drink to you in good heath
To your kindness full of wealth
I drink to you in good health

Eternally the first and the last
I will remember you in times past
Eternally the first and the last

Ἑστία ἐστι*

by Edward P. Butler

In Plato's *Cratylus*, the famous discussion of esoteric etymologies of the names of the Gods begins with that of Hestia: Socrates asks, "Shall we begin with any other but Hestia, as is customary?" (401b). He proceeds to justify this cultic priority accorded to Hestia by the similarity between the name 'Hestia' and words for 'being' in Greek: *esti*, 'is', and *ousia*, participle of the verb 'to be', which the philosophical tradition has translated as 'substance' or 'essence', which Socrates notes is pronounced by some *essia*: "For it would be reasonable to sacrifice to Hestia first before all the Gods for those who named the essence of all things *essia*," (401d). The etymologies of the *Cratylus* are by no means intended to be etymologies in the modern linguistic sense, but rather to unfold diverse possible trains of association of sound and meaning that might capture the human contribution to the theophanic experience in which a god is first encountered and named. The impression, therefore, of Hestia's primordial theophany upon those "elevated and subtle minds" (401b) was such, according to Plato, as to make them think of being itself. Insofar as philosophy, in one of its key senses, is the science of being *qua* being, Hestia may be said to be one of the primary divine patrons of philosophy. Being itself is a power of Hestia's insofar as essence is the common hearth of all things, the home of all things that are and that come to be, making them known and bringing them to knowledge in its light, and perfecting them in its warmth.

Eldest daughter of Kronos, whose name in the *Cratylus* evokes the 'pure intellect' (*katharos noûs*, 396b), Hestia remains closest to him as first ingested and last disgorged. Kronian intelligence is pure precisely because it leaves nothing in experience alien and unassimilated, but takes its offspring back up into itself; as Proclus says, this intellect "is turned back upon itself, seeing as it turns even those that have proceeded forth from it back to itself, embraces them and establishes them stably in itself," (Proclus, *In Platonis Cratylum commentaria,* ed. Pasquali, p. 57.7-9). In much the same way, Hestia "is said to remain in herself, since she keeps her virginity immaculate and is the cause of *identity* for all things," (*In Crat.* 79.15-17). In this regard, Hestia seems to hold a Kronian sovereignty irreducible to that divided among Kronos' sons Zeus, Poseidon and Hades, even aside from the fact that Kronos' sons obtain his sovereignty as a result of rebellious action. The idea of Hestia's conservation and transmission of this particular aspect of Kronos' sovereignty in this particular fashion also offers to shed light on a quality of Hestia's upon which scholars have often remarked, namely the paucity of mythic narrative attached to her. Hestia's dearth of myth is often treated in a rather trivializing fashion as a function of her sphere of activity in the home, but this hardly follows. Rather, if we have an appreciation for the *ontological* status of mythic narrative, as that eternal activity of the gods which brings about the intellective articulation of the cosmos, then Hestia's minimal engagement in myth would pertain to her carrying forward into the successive stages of cosmogony the specific Kronian potency of *self-identity*, insofar as this is a property diminished through the establishment of many particular relationships, relations which determine who someone is *for* this one and *for* that one.

In this fashion Proclus explains that the phases of divine activity prior to Kronos "do not possess the qualities of 'being-in-oneself' and 'being-in-another', but this begins from Kronos. The quality of 'being-in-oneself' belongs to Hestia, that of 'being-in-another' to Hera," (*In Crat.* 80.3-6). Proclus emphasizes this reciprocity between the powers of Hestia and of Hera in another connection in his commentary on the *Cratylus*. When Socrates initially connects essence, *ousia*, to Hestia, he explains that some dialects pronounce *ousia* as *essia* while others pronounce it as *ôsia* (401c), and that those who pronounce it in the latter way would be inclined to think of *ôthoun*, 'to push, drive', from which come forms like *ôsis*, 'thrusting, pushing'; and hence "those who call it *ôsia* would believe almost like Heraclitus that all beings pass away and nothing remains stable. So the cause and principle of these men is *drive* [*to ôthoun*], from which it has rightly been named *ôsia*," (401d). This 'driving' power of Hestia's is associated by Proclus with a mutual participation between Hestia and Hera. Hestia and Hera, he explains, "are of the same rank as the demiurgic causes," i.e., the three sovereigns Zeus, Poseidon and Hades.

> From herself Hestia provides unabating permanence, the establishment [of beings] in themselves and indissoluble essence, while Hera provides procession and multiplication into lower levels of being, and is the life-creating font of the reason-principles and mother of the generative powers … [T]hose that have looked to the mode of existence proper to her say that Hestia has been named from *essia*, while those that have looked to her power of motion and bearing life, the power which exists in her from Hera, give her the name *ôsia* because she is cause of drive [*ôsis*]. For all the divine entities are in all, and coordinate entities especially participate in each other and subsist in

each other. Therefore, each of both the demiurgic and life-bearing orders possesses its very essence, which comes from Hestia, by participation; the revolutions of the planets in heaven derive their constancy from her; and the poles and the cardinal points are allotted their eternal fixedness from her. (*In Crat.* 79.8-28)

As all of the gods, who in their existence (*hyparxis*) are *hyperousios*, that is, supra-essential or prior to essence as such, participate in essence nevertheless through Hestia, so Hestia, participating in Hera, embodies in her *own* essence a power of giving life and motion to things.

This activity of essence as causing life and motion in its own right, which comes from the divine cause of essentiality, Hestia, participating in her youngest sister,[1] in addition to its significance for the intellectual project of a science of essences, which must for its own sake therefore partake as well of life and of change,[2] also has significance relative to what Plato says about Hestia in another dialogue, the *Phaedrus*. For there, Plato explains that when the other Olympians drive their chariots through the heavens, that is, when they enter into psychical procession — horses and chariots as always symbols of the work of soul and of ensoulment — that "Hestia alone remains in the dwelling of the Gods" (247a). Understood in a trivial and anthropomorphic sense as pertaining to her withdrawn character, this passage is the most likely source for the crass joke of Robert Graves' which many have credulously accepted as ancient doctrine, namely that Hestia surrendered her place among the Olympians so that Dionysos could be counted among the twelve. In point of fact, the notion of twelve canonical Olympians is as flexible as the canonical 'ennead' of Egyptian theology, which consists of almost any assortment of nine deities, or even of a smaller or larger number according to a literal head count, while retaining its ideal ninefold character.

Instead, we ought to interpret the special activity accorded to Hestia here by Plato in light of what Plato has said about her in the *Cratylus*, that is, as pertaining to the status of *essence* in virtue of the manner of its production by Hestia. The procession of the Gods in their vehicles is inseparable from their attracting mortal souls into their train as their followers, and this fascination with whichever God they 'follow' is how mortal souls gain their innate grasp of the intelligible which they in turn sow in the world through their acts of love (*Phaedrus* 250b, 252c-253c).[3] Hestia alone of the Olympians does not sow in this fashion, however, because as the source of essence itself, it is she who secures the place or *topos* of really-existing being (ibid., 247c-d), so that the striving of mortal souls to grasp the nature of divine being can have a determinate object. As securing through her activity the *oikos* of the Gods, Hestia ensures that the divine banquet (247a) where the Gods reciprocally experience each other's divine virtue is itself concrete, and not reducible to the individual divine perspectives, that there is a hearth, a center in itself, and not only the polycentric manifold of the Gods themselves.

Hestia's own followers, therefore, have a path distinct from that of the followers of the other Olympians. Plato does not mention them specifically when he discusses the kinds of *eros* manifested by the followers of diverse Gods in procession (252c-253b), I would argue because he is not concerned in this dialogue with the activities of concrete institution in the world which would attract the *eros* of those souls who experience from afar Hestia's attraction. Plato makes no specific mention here of the followers of Hermes, either, and this may be more significant than mere silence would ordinarily suggest. Hermes is paired with Hestia in remarkable fashion in *Homeric Hymn* 29, where Hermes and Hestia are urged to "dwell together in the glorious houses" of humans inasmuch as "both of you know the noble works of earth-dwellers" (11-13). Hermes and Hestia, then, are both in some sense to be found within the terrestrial sphere; and this is the subject of an essay by Jean-Pierre Vernant.[4] He argues that

> To Hestia belongs the world of the interior, the enclosed, the stable, the retreat of the human group within itself; to Hermes, the outside world, opportunity, movement, interchange with others. It could be said that, by virtue of their polarity, the Hermes-Hestia couple represents the marked tension in the archaic conception of space: space requires a center, a nodal point, with a special value, from which all directions, all qualitatively different, may be channeled and defined; yet, at the same time, space is the medium of movement, implying the possibility of transition and passage from any point to another. (161)

As the polarity that defines terrestrial spatiality in its human dimension, Hestia and Hermes are somehow outside the *Phaedrus*' system of heavenly (Ouranian) fructification of the lives of mortal souls — in which connection it is useful to recall Hestia's immunity to Aphrodite's power (*Homeric Hymn* 5, 21-35), the wide range of which expresses the sovereignty Aphrodite inherits from her father Ouranos, while Hestia, as I have argued, in some sense bears the Kronian sovereignty intact to Earth.

Reading more deeply into Plato's account of

Hestia in the *Phaedrus* in conjunction with what he says about her in the *Cratylus*, the focus for the soul's attraction to Hestia would not be a discrete psychical vehicle of hers, at least not in the sense in which it is for the other Olympians. For Hestia does not establish a revolution through the ideal motion of her chariot, which is the same as to note the paucity of mythic narrative in connection to her, for the myths express these motions or cycles of the Gods, and the mortal soul's fascination its participation in these intelligible motions. Rather, the mortal soul must be attracted to Hestia and partake of her power of 'essencing' through the essence of its *own* vehicle, that is, through the very materiality of that soul's incarnation.

Plato would have counted on his readers' intimate familiarity with the *amphidromia*, in which the newborn child is carried around the hearth and laid upon the ground of the home as their introduction into the *oikos* — the opposite, as Vernant points out (188f), of the laying down of the child in a wild place in the practice of exposure, which leads in myth to their adoption by a shepherd or other representative of Hermes. In this fashion it would have been available to his reader to grasp that everyone, purely by virtue of birth, participates in Hestia's revolution or *periphora* (*Phaedrus* 247c), and hence it would be redundant for Hestia to make a separate *periphora*. We can discern a similar symbolism exhibited in Hestia's civic functions in equalizing citizens within the Prytaneum, the hearth of the *polis*.

These reflections draw us back to the hearth as the site for the negotiation of the categories of insider and outsider or, ontologically, essence and accident. Hestia's role at the hearth both recognizes the distinctness of households and families, as well as the possibility of these units opening themselves to incorporate the outsider, whether permanently through marriage, when the daughter who tended her family's hearth takes a new home with her husband, or temporarily as guests, through *hestiasis*, receiving at one's hearth or 'entertaining', for "without you [Hestia] mortals hold no banquet, where one does not duly pour sweet wine in offering to Hestia both first and last," (*Homeric Hymn* 29, 4-6). As Vernant puts it, "The center symbolized by Hestia … not only defines a closed and isolated world but also presupposes, as a corollary, other, analogous centers," (174).

As mistress of the *oikos*, Hestia also has a specifically 'economic' (*oiko-nomos*) function. As Hestia Tamia, guardian of the stores, of the accumulated wealth — another sense of *ousia* — of the *oikos*, whether conceived as the familial household or the *polis* unit, Hestia at once provides the possibility of the market activity that is Hermes' domain, and limits it, inasmuch as not everything is for sale. As Vernant again remarks,

> Since the term *oikos* has both a family and a territorial meaning, it is easy to understand the undercurrents that hamper purchases and sales in the case of family landed property (*klêros*) in a fully mercantile economy. Equally comprehensible is the refusal to grant strangers the right to own 'the city's' land: this is the privilege and right of the autochthonous citizen. (171)

It is in Hestia's power both to endorse such claims of authentic belonging to an *oikos*, and to recast those boundaries, so that the guest becomes a member of the family, the alien a citizen. From a strictly economic point of view, Hestia thus presides both over the transposition of living substance into 'capital', as seen in a sacrifice to Zeus Polieus, 'guardian of the *polis*', in which the price of the victim is publicly declared and paid by the citizens, not to its owner, but to Hestia (ibid., 183),[5] *but also* over the conservation of substance by withholding or sheltering it from commodification. Philosophically, Socrates refers in the *Theaetetus* (160e) to subjecting the intuitions elicited through his 'midwifery' to an *amphidromia*, the circle of argumentative examination, to determine whether it is to be 'raised' or 'exposed'. This is what distinguishes Socrates from a sophist who merely traffics in ideas without concern for their truth, their relationship to essence, *ousia*, but only for the price they may command in the marketplace of persuasion, another of the powers of Hermes.

Proclus' comments on Hestia's power of causing motion in her own right see this potency as emerging in and through Hestia's experience of her sister Hera within herself; and Hera does produce a discrete psychical vehicle and cosmic revolution ("And those who followed after Hera seek a kingly [*basilikon*] nature," (*Phaedrus* 253b)). It would be this potency, therefore, its nature bound up in the foundation of the temporal power structures through which Hera exercises her particular sovereignty,[6] that the peculiar devotee of Hestia would appropriate, its ambivalent status corresponding to the lack in Hellenic cult of an office corresponding to the Vestals of Rome. On the other hand, Hestia is paired in *Homeric Hymn* 24 with Apollo at Delphi: "Hestia, you who tend the holy house of the lord Apollo, the Far-shooter at goodly Pytho, with soft oil dripping ever from your locks, come now into this house, come, having one mind with Zeus the all-wise," (trans. H. G. Evelyn-White). Hestia's union with the mind of Zeus here comes together with her power over the very cultic center for the Hellenic world. Plato says that Apollo "from his seat in the middle and at the very navel of the earth delivers his interpretation … for all humanity … of the religion of their fathers [*patriois*]" (*Republic*

427c). Hestia, as the Goddess at the center, presides at Delphi over the religious center of the entire world. But Plato is not so parochial as to be unaware that all peoples do not, in fact, acknowledge Delphi as the site of such divine authority. It is not this that matters, but rather the *openness* of Delphi, its universal *appeal* that grants it this universality, which is not an assertion of hegemony but an invitation, an empty seat at the hearth for the guest or suitor, as the case may be, who wishes to partake for a time or for all time in the divine intelligence embodied in Hellenic civilization itself.

Notes
* *Hestia esti*, 'Hestia is'
1) Hera is twin sister of Zeus according to Lactantius (*Divine Institutes* I, chap. 14), while others make her out to be the eldest; these relations being non-exclusive among the Gods, it is clearly as youngest sister that Hera manifests her power of motion, while it is insofar as she is eldest that she is queen (*basileia*).
2) As well as, perhaps, a *determinate sovereignty* of some sort as falling under Hera's sway, on which see more below.
3) See "Plato's Gods and the Way of Ideas", *Diotima: Review of Philosophical Research* 39, 2011 (Hellenic Society for Philosophical Studies,

Athens), pp. 73-87.

4) "Hestia-Hermes: The Religious Expression of Space and Movement in Ancient Greece," in *Myth and Thought among the Greeks* (New York: Zone Books, 2006), pp. 157-196.

5) Compare the divinatory rite from Pharai discussed by Vernant (192), which involves laying upon Hestia's altar a *domestic coin*, and then whispering in the ear of Hermes' statue the inquiry, the God's answer coming to the querent through the first voice they hear after leaving the agora and uncovering his ears. Here, the monetizing of the divination through Hestia is symbolically identified with the randomness, anonymity, in short *externality,* through which Hermes delivers his response.

6) On which see "Queen of *Kinêsis*: Understanding Hera," in *Queen of Olympos: A Devotional Anthology for Hera and Iuno*, ed. Lykeia (Asheville, NC: Bibliotheca Alexandrina, 2013), pp. 126-148.

Hearth and Fire

by Chelsea Luellon Bolton

The domestic sphere I rule
For I am divine;
I am the fire, roaring in the hearth
I am the fire in the hearts of those who dwell in the
        household.
I am the sacred fire lit in temples and on shrines.
I am the hearth and home.
All is sacred under Me.
Do you see?
I am the candle flame which is lit
on every altar, on every shrine
in all holy places, I dwell.
I am the light and flame of the heart and hearth.
I am the roaring fire,
I am the warmth of flame.
All who worship Me, do so first.
For I am the fire which consumes the sacrifice to all
        the Gods.
All rituals, all offerings are sacred to Me,
since I am the gateway for them to reach the Gods.
I am the roaring fire.
I am the warmth of flame.
I am the Goddess of the people
for I live where they reside;
in temples, in cities and in homes.
I watch over them, near and far.

I am the flame carried from home to home
when one takes a wife.
I am the flame which connects families and
        households.
As I connect cities and shrines through the candles
        lit within them.
Shrine to shrine, temple to temple.
I reside in them all.

I am the patron of women and those who maintain
        their homes.
The abode is where I reside.
Cleaning, cooking and other domestic duties
are under My domain.
These are sacred to Me.
All households.
All homes
are My dwelling.

All libations are mine.
The first and last.
The offerings are given to Me
due to My honor and My place.
I am the hearth in every home.
I am the fire in every spark.
I am the candle flame on the mantle of shrines.

I am the Goddess of the hearth and home.
I reside in them all.

For I connect all people, families, temples and
	shrines.
Through flame.
Through ritual.
Through homes.

I am where they reside.
I am the veiled Goddess
holding the flame.
I am the crowned lady, wielding the fire.
I am bathed in white because I am holy.
I am the Goddess of fire.
I am the Goddess of flame.
I am the lady of fire in the hearth.
I am the holy Goddess of hallowed space.
All shrines are mine. All temples are mine.
For I am there as well.
When one visits a God or Goddess, one visits me
	as well.
For I am there.
In every shrine.

Athena Ergane and Hera and I,
all rule this work.
But I am the one who is the flame and fire.
And I am the one who lights the hearth.
And I am the roaring fire.
And I am the warmth of flame.
These belong to Me.

I am Hestia of the hearth and home.
I am the Goddess who dwells in all these places.
Anytime a candle is lit, I am present.
Anytime a hymn is sung, I am there.
Anytime a prayer is uttered, I come swiftly.

I am the Goddess who answers the prayers of the
      people.
I come when I am called.
I stay where I am welcome.
I reside in the home and the hearth
and the flame.
See Me and know Me, for who I am.
I am Hestia.
I am in all flame,
all homes and shrines.
Light the fire
and I come forth.

The Tale of Erinna and Philôn

by Rebecca Buchanan

[Translator's Note: it is a sad truth recognized by classical scholars that the vast majority of texts produced by ancient authors have been lost to us; most to time and apathy, a few to deliberate destruction. Where *The Nursery Tales of the Wife of Leander*[1] falls is difficult to determine. There are scattered references to the collection in, for example, Drusus' *Works of Excellence* (first century)[2] and Saint Fulgora's *Against Pagan Education* (fourth century)[3], and Mirzam ibn Fahladin's *Great Works of the Ptolemaic Court*[4] suggests that a nearly complete text survived as late as the seventh century of the common era. Sadly, only "The Tale of Erinna and Philôn" remains to us whole.]

Long ago, in the days before Apollo and Poseidon built the walls of Troy, there lived a poor widow and her son. The widow, Erinna was her name, washed and sewed the clothing of her neighbors to earn what coin she could. Her son, Philôn was his name, performed what labors were needed, great and small alike, from picking rocks out of the field to chopping wood to cleaning stables. And though their neighbors paid Erinna and Philôn for these tasks, and though they were necessary tasks, nonetheless their neighbors one and all looked down upon Erinna and her son.

Despite the contempt of their neighbors, Erinna and Philôn remained proud, for they knew that what they did was necessary work, and that work kept their bellies full and their hearth lit and the roof over their heads tight against the rain and the cold.

Now it just so happened one day that great Zeus returned to Olympus from one of his many wanderings. And he complained endlessly to any and all who would listen as to the wretchedness and miserliness of humanity, and of how the kindness was bleeding slowly from their hearts.

Sweet Hestia, sitting beside the hearth at the heart of Olympus, did not believe Zeus' tales. For the hearth she tended touched every hearth in the world, and through its flames gentle Hestia could see and hear all the hurts and worries and desires of the mortal world. And she told great Zeus, but he, still angry, only waved his hand and lightning crashed through the halls of Olympus.

Boldly, wise Hestia rose to her feet and vowed to prove great Zeus wrong. And so she took up a tongue of flame and wove it into an old cloak, dirty and ragged. And she shuttered the light of her own divinity and made her appearance into that of an old woman, stricken with hunger and disease, and she descended from Olympus to the world below.

And she walked from house to house, from town to town, from city to city, old cloak around her shoulders. And she knocked on every door, asking for shelter, for food, for drink. And though some offered her drink, and a few offered her food, none would offer her a place at their hearth.

Gentle Hestia continued to wander, her heart beginning to fill with sadness.

And then, as a heavy rain fell, she came to the village where Erinna lived with her son. And she went from door to door, limbs shaking with cold, her cloak wrapped tight over her stooping shoulders. And every door was closed in her face; not a one offered her even a bit of bread or a sip of water.

Until at last she came to poor Erinna and Philôn's home. Tiny though it was, with only a single table and two chairs and straw for sleeping upon, the hearth inside was burning bright and warm. And Erinna welcomed the stranger into her home, and Philôn gave her his chair to rest her weary feet. And they offered her what little bread they had, and soup, too, serving it in plain wooden bowls, and the last of the summer fruits. And when night fell at last, they offered their guest the bed of straw, and Erinna and Philôn laid down themselves on the hard stone beside the hearth.

Gentle Hestia was well pleased.

In the dark of the night, with only wide-eyed Selene to witness, Hestia set aside her old ragged cloak and her mortal form and returned again to Olympus. And there she told great Zeus and all the shining assembly of Gods what she had seen and what she had heard and what she had found: that there was still kindness and hospitality in the world.

Zeus was silent for long moments. When he at last lifted his great head, it was to ask gentle Hestia what boon she requested of him for Erinna and Philôn, who had shown her such graciousness. And the blessing that Hestia requested was a simple one: that their cupboards always be well stocked with bread and meat and fruits and milk, that they might have enough for all when they next welcomed a stranger into their home.

And great Zeus agreed, and to this sweet Hestia added a blessing of her own: their hearth would always burn warm and bright, through even the coldest of winter nights.

And so when Helios rose above the edge of the world, Erinna and Philôn discovered that their guest was nowhere to be found; but their cupboards were filled with good things to eat, and, no matter how much they ate, the cupboards remained full. The same was true of their hearth, which never needed fresh wood to continue burning.

Erinna and Philôn continued to sew and wash for their neighbors, continued to clear rocks and chop wood and clean stables. The coin they earned, though, they used not for themselves, but for the many poor and sick who came to their door;

for word spread from village to village, from town to town, and from city to city that the home of Erinna and Philôn was a blessed and welcoming one, where the hearth always burned warm and bright.

Notes
1) The exact title and the identity of the author are unknown. Given the nature of publishing and the position of women in ancient Greek society, and what little biographical information has survived, the following seems likely: the wife of Leander lived in Byblos (modern-day Beirut) sometime in the first century BCE. She produced this collection of tales for her own children, either writing them down herself or, more likely, reciting them to a professional scribe. These were then copied and passed out among her friends and family. More copies were produced, at least one of which eventually found its way to Alexandria where, centuries later, Mirzam ibn Fahladin mistakenly assumed it had actually been created at the Ptolemaic court.
2) *Works of Excellence* by Drusus (translated by Miriam Lester), Harridon Publishing, 1937. Drusus' collection consists of lists of moral precepts (e.g., temperance, justice, perseverance, et cetera) followed by references to texts which demonstrate these virtues. Thanks to Drusus, we know that *The Nursery Tales of the Wife of Leander* originally

consisted of thirteen stories, each featuring a different deity and a different virtue. He explicitly identifies three of them: ancestral devotion (Mnemosyne), truthfulness (Helios), and courage (Herakles). Interestingly, he makes no reference to "The Tale of Erinna and Philôn" (hospitality).

3) Scholars have long debated the existence of Saint Fulgora. Considering that Fulgora was the Roman goddess of lightning, and that the saint was said to have been saved from a horrible death by a bolt out of the blue, it is entirely possible that he (note the gender change) is fictitious. There is no denying the existence of *Against Pagan Education*, however, which argues that Christians should avoid any and all Pagan texts, even those which celebrate virtues recognized by Christianity. *Against Pagan Education* contains the only surviving ancient reference to "The Tale of Erinna and Philôn," in which Fulgora (or someone writing as him) argues that it is meant not to model the virtue of hospitality, but to trick gullible Christians into inviting demons into their homes. See Gustavus Swan's translation (The Laurel Academy Press, 1948).

4) *Great Works of the Ptolemaic Court* by Mirzam ibn Fahladin (trans. Carl Keane), Stanley House Publishing, 1933, pp. 110-111. We know of one more story thanks to ibn Fahladin: that of Iris, and the virtue of keeping true to one's oath. A curious choice on ibn Fahladin's part, but there it is.

[Author's Note: no such collection as *The Nursery Tales of the Wife of Leander* exists, or is known to have existed. It is, true, however, that very few texts survive from the ancient world.]

Invocation by Frederic Lord Leighton

The First of February

by Eric Paul Shaffer

The fire blazed in that cottage, summer, fall, spring,
        no matter the wood within nor weather
without, but for the first of February. That day,
        she watched the fire burn low,
    beat out the gleaming embers,

and let the hearth cool. She spent the morning
        scraping soot from stone
    and swept a year of ashes across the floor,
over the threshold, from the steps into the yard.
    Noon was cold meat and bread, then back

bent once more, she chipped and scraped
        till the place was clean, carried in five
fresh-split limbs for the iron frame, and arranged
the tinder and kindling. The cottage was cold,
    and she donned a sweater,

then a cloak and stiff leather shoes for the frozen
        road before she set out beneath a silver sky.
           When evening drew on, she returned
from the village, where in the square,
    the bonfire had burned since dawn.

On a bit of tinder, she cupped the spark
she had carried home and brought the flame to life
        with her breath. Kneeling on stone,
she coaxed fire forth once more. Gray smoke rose,
        the chill left the air,

walls warmed, and her home glowed with light
    from the same flame kindled anew
        that day on every village hearth.

Hestia's Tale
by Melia Brokaw

A large man sits staring at his small campfire muttering under his breath. He looks tired and travel-worn, with no extra flesh on his frame. Even his eyes look weary and low. Next to him is a mostly empty pack and a club.

"May I join you?" says a female voice. As she speaks, the once small campfire blazes up into a bonfire. In the dancing flames, there stands a woman, looking calmly at the traveler whose initial surprise is quickly hidden.

"Isn't my fire, your own?" he replies a bit testily.

Softly she laughs, "Yes, but neither would I wish to intrude where I am not wanted."

With a grand sweeping gesture, Herakles stands and bows, "Well, my divine aunt, be welcome at my temporary hearth. Only the finest seat will do for you." Quickly he rolls a large stump into the circle of light cast by the flame.

Hestia, youngest and eldest sister of Zeus, goddess of the hearth steps out of the blaze which then returns to its original size. She is a beautiful goddess with long, curly, bright red hair, barely restrained by its braid. She is dressed in a pale blue chiton that is almost completely hidden by her variegated flame-colored himation. The goddess sits herself on the stump as if it was the grandest of seats in the hall of the Olympians.

"How can I be of service, my lady?" he asks, sitting on the ground at her feet.

"Is it not possible that I just wished to visit my nephew?" she answers. Seeing the look of disbelief on his face, she sighs. "No, you are right. I want you to help me to honor a request in return for helping you with your next labor. I know of one who will know where to find a very particular apple, from a very particular tree. And I want you to do it all without ever mentioning my visit to you."

"What do you get out of this?" says the wary demi-god.

"Nothing ... really. A sense of justice served. Maybe a little revenge upon my brother, your father."

"I don't understand."

"No. No, I don't suppose you do. Many don't. Many forget that I have a past and an opinion. Since when has a flame ever been passive? Even the smallest spark can destroy a town. I am ignored just because I do not choose to strive for power as my siblings have done. I have all the power I need or want." She quietly stares into the flame. "Let me tell you a tale. Well, more like a series of tales. Some of it you may know. Some of it will be a surprise. Quiet and passive? Not and survive this bunch!"

I: Birth

As you know from the tales, I am the first born of my parents. Father in his "wisdom" decided to swallow each of us at birth to prevent the takeover of his kingdom. What is never discussed is that I am much older than the rest. I was alone for a long time, because Mother was very angry with Father for swallowing me. I'm actually surprised she had any more children with him, but all this I only learned later. At the time, it was just the natural order of things to have children falling from above. As they arrived or shortly thereafter I named them with names you will not recognize.

My first memory is of darkness. Not the warmth of my mother, not my father's voice, just darkness. I was alone. There was no one to answer my cries, no one to hold me or feed me, no bed, no toys, no food, no light. There was only me and my swaddling clothes. I had no knowledge of where I was or why I was there. I didn't know anything about anything. All I knew is that there was rumbling from time to time and that food and drink would arrive from above. I won't tell you how long I cried or how long it took me to pull myself together. I can't even say I was lonely because this was all I knew.

I spent a lot of time in contemplation. It started out as trying to see something without, but eventually I moved within as there was nothing to see. It was during that time that I found my inner spark. Everyone has one, but few have the time, luxury or patience to find it. I eventually learned to pull that spark outside of myself. The first time I did it, I lost control and Father had his first bout of heartburn. Yes, Father from then on had quite the issue with heartburn.

So I had light for the first time and it was painful to look upon. Eventually I learned to control it. Rarely did I light up my surroundings, because really there wasn't anything worth seeing. Generally I gave myself just enough light for comfort, for a sense of something that I didn't know how to define.

The end of my solitude came when what dropped down from above was not food, but something else. Something that squalled and kicked and mewed. I must say, it took me longer than I would like to admit to investigate that bundle. As you may have guessed, that something was a child, a sibling, though I didn't know it at the time. I named the child Xanthe, for her hair reminded me of the golden part of my flame.

Now you may wonder how I learned to talk, how I learned language. I'm not sure. I think some part of my brain absorbed and translated the rumblings of my father's speech into something intelligible that I didn't need until Xanthe arrived.

There were times that I enjoyed having another around and other times that I longed for my solitude. Yet I did what was needed. I cared for the child, gave her the comfort that I never had. There were still no toys, no comfort of home. Only me and my flame but we made the best of it.

Then the next child came. Xanthe was old enough that she took to mothering the child, as I mothered her, only she was better at it than I was. I was content to let her as it gave her something to do and meant I didn't need to entertain her as often. I teasingly started calling her Demeter, "the mother," because of her actions.

The child I called Pais, "girl," partially to differentiate her from Xanthe and partially because I had no idea what else to call her. As Pais grew older, there were times I had to deal with their bickering, for the youngest of us had quite a temper, but for the most part we were a pretty peaceful trio.

Then the next child arrived from above. This one was a male child who was so moody and different from the girls. He didn't take to Xanthe's mothering too well. He'd often push her away and sit by my flame, peering in, looking for what I don't know. Peace and quiet maybe, as the girls were quite shrill at times. It took us awhile to name the boy, as nothing we thought of seemed suitable. Eventually he was named Aidein, one who makes invisible, for his tendency to ignore Xanthe and Pais to the point that they'd wonder if they had become invisible to him.

I was actually thankful when the next child arrived. Another male, whom I hoped would pull

Aidein out of himself, but it was not to be. Where Aidein was silent, this child was loud. Where Aidein was still, this child was constantly moving. Where Aidein avoided Xanthe, this child would follow and cling to her if she allowed it. We named him Enosis, "shaker," for his seemingly constant movement would shake our residence. He had to have given Father quite the unsettled stomach.

Enosis was also quite a bit older than the other children were when they arrived. He had a few memories which he would recount the few times we could get him to sit still. I liked and hated those times. I liked hearing about Mother, but it would upset the other children, especially Xanthe. They resented not having similar memories of her and the outside world, but for Xanthe it put her in conflict with wanting to mother, and yet be mothered by a woman of whom she had no memory.

By this time, I was really longing for my solitude. While it was nice to have company, there was no way to escape either. I loved them all, but there was so much noise and they were everywhere. They were growing and the space around us wasn't. Instead it was getting rather crowded. One could hardly move without hitting someone in the process. Then the rock came. When it fell, it narrowly missed hitting Pais on the head and on its up-bounce it knocked Enosis clean off his feet. It took some time to calm both of them down. Pais was hysterical and Enosis indignant. Afterwards, we just stared at this cloth-wrapped rock in confounded amazement, wondering what the meaning of it was. There were no more children after that and nothing changed for the longest time. We all continued to grow, and the available space continued to shrink.

II. Rebirth

The quietest time since the others arrived was when the glowing green mist rained down upon us. Our surroundings immediately started to heave and a female voice pronounced "The last shall be first, the first shall be last." To my horrified eyes, the others, whom I had cared for, mediated among, and loved, became paralyzed and somehow folded in on themselves. They didn't seem to be in pain, just somehow less.

I flared up in my panic to dispel the mist, only to have a voice in my head tell me to calm myself. "Your foster children are no longer yours to care for; the time has come for rebirth. Prepare them and prepare yourself. Move the mist to those who need more, but remember to save some for yourself. Quickly now."

I found that by a combination of scooping and wafting I was able to move the mist despite the constant movement of the floor and walls. I took most of what I could reach from the once-swaddled rock — which was already floating upwards — and slathered Enosis with it. Even paralyzed, he vibrated intensely. As Enosis started to rise upwards his vibrating increased, causing him to sink. I had to again slather him with mist while attempting to calm him. This time I gathered the necessary mist from Aidein, who stared at me morosely as I did so. Enosis continued rising up, but I was afraid to look. Instead I turned back to Aidein, who was not as far under the mist's effects now. I kissed him on the forehead, which seemed to sooth him somewhat, as his eyes closed and he relaxed. Then he, too, started to rise.

    Pais was thankfully completely under the mist's spell. Although a lovely and intelligent girl, she was also the most high-strung and temperamental of the bunch. She, too, started to rise, following after Aidein. I turned to Xanthe, and saw that the mist was starting to dissipate. I had yet to coat myself. I evened out the mist around this first child, taking only minute amounts where it was thickest and then gathering up what was left in our surroundings. Xanthe seemed to patiently wait with no struggle apparent, a determined look upon her face. As she started to rise, I began coating myself with what was left.

    There wasn't enough. Try as I might there wasn't enough mist to cover more than the lower half of my body. That wasn't enough to even make me float. I was going to be stuck here all alone. As I crumbled in on my grief, I heard the voice again.

    "Change child. Change into your flame!"

Change? I thought. *How?*

"That flame is a part of you that you project outwards. Become one with that flame, but don't tamp it down to mute it. Let it surround and transform you. Let go of your form and change! *Now*!"

And I did. I don't know how it happened that first time, but I did it. As a flame I rose from Father's throat, scorching it along the way. I was caught in a kettle by the owner of the voice who spoke with me. Father was too incapacitated to prevent any of his children from being removed from his presence, but I'm told his eyes were blazing hot with anger.

I remained as a flame for some time until a teacher could be found to instruct me in how to turn myself back. It wasn't as natural as one would think for someone like me. Some of it was reluctance on my own part. The world was so big and loud and contentious. Metis, for that is whose voice it was, kept me with her, telling me to take my time. She said I had a place in this world and that I would always be honored for the care I gave my siblings.

For the time being, I was set in the central area of whatever abode the others gathered in, and was generally forgotten. I learned much about the happenings of the family in this fashion due to the soothing heat of my flame. My "foster children," as Metis called them, were used to it and so naturally gathered around me. Zeus, in this manner, followed the lead of the others.

III. Transition

The tales make it sound as if the time that followed the disgorgement was rather cut and dried. So and so went here, so and so got this power. It wasn't nearly so smooth. There was never any doubt of who was going to be the head of the family, but everything else only fell into place gradually. I'll say one thing for Zeus: he's always had good insight into his siblings, and uses that advantage as it suits him. He often plays a long game that no one else ever sees. I'll briefly tell you how things turned out.

Xanthe's tendency to mother everyone quickly became an irritant to her siblings. They all wanted to stretch themselves and she kept trying to contain them. Once she started in on Zeus, who was not used to being mothered, she quickly found herself relegated as an overseer for Gaia who had too much to do to take care of all the smaller details of her ecology. To my amusement, Zeus chose her nickname, Demeter, as her official title.

Without Xanthe around, Pais floundered, becoming an irritant in everyone's hide. War was brewing and while the girl could be very argumentative, she wasn't a warrior. She could, however, mope and hold a grudge very well. When Zeus wasn't trying to manage his siblings or the threat our father posed, he was spending time with Metis. She is the one who suggested that Pais be sent to our aunt and uncle. There the contentious girl could grow up without hindrance and out of the shadows of the others.

Enosis never quite got over being contained by the green mist, or Father's belly for that matter. He needs a lot of room and his tendency to bounce around was quite destructive. It was accidentally discovered that large bodies of water did well to cushion this tendency. Just as Gaia needed help, so did Oceanus need an overseer. Enosis volunteered and found that he liked the watery realm quite well. It was at that time that he took on the title of Poseidon.

Aidein, well he could never be found by the others between meals and martial training. I always knew where he was, however. He was taking advantage of his need to be alone and away from his chaotic siblings. He liked the quiet of caves and still waters. Aidein rarely spoke, but when he did he was concise, and had wisdom beyond his years. His lack of attention to politics is what caused Aidein to end up with Haides as his duty. I don't think he minded too much, though. In time he became so associated with his realm that some thought that Haides was his name.

As for me, it was left to Prometheus to woo me back into corporal form. I don't know why he cared or why he was interested, but he was. He'd come sit by my flame and chat. Sometimes he'd tell me stories. Sometimes he'd be just silent. Well, the day he talked me out of the flame, the family decided to throw a feast to celebrate.

It was at this feast that Prometheus and Enosis started trying to verbally outdo each other. Somehow my name came up in their conversation. Suddenly I had both males vying for my body, swearing to father the most children on me. (Remember, marriage hadn't been invented yet.) Oh no, I wasn't going to have any of that. I'm not a pawn to be moved around to further their egos or their houses.

The tales say that I touched Zeus on the head stating a vow to remain a maiden all my days. That isn't exactly what happened. But then the tales also say it was Apollo and Poseidon that competed, which wasn't possible as Apollo hadn't even been born yet. What happened was that I lost my temper. I was a bonfire of indignation and I roared that nothing and no one could make me whelp any children.

"I have raised all the children I'm going to raise!" I yelled.

The women tried to cajole me and the men tried to woo me, but I was having none of it. There were many scorched fingers and clothing that needed replacing before it was decided that I was serious.

Zeus was rather amused by all this for reasons I've never understood. When he tired of the commotion, Zeus decreed that I may stay a maid all my days and that my place is the hearth, the center of both homes and temples. I was not given *a* home, but all homes. Wherever gatherings take place, whether mundane or divine, that is my place. Since I was both the first and the last born, he decreed that I was due the honor of receiving both the first and last offerings in payment for all that I had sacrificed during those dark days of dwelling within our father.

Strangely enough, Prometheus was very pleased by the pronouncement of Zeus, especially since he was one of the males that wanted to claim me. It was then that I learned that Zeus is not the only one who plays a long game, but what Prometheus' game is, I've never quite understood. Maybe his foretelling ability is better than generally known. I really don't know.

IV. Creation

In time my family became bored, and looked for something more. I'll spare you the tedious details, but eventually animals and mortals were created.

These beings were introduced to Gaia's surface in a logical fashion designated by Zeus, but the distributing of gifts and abilities was left to Prometheus and his brother, Epimetheus. I'm not clear why or how this happened, but the results were less than positive.

Between the two of them it was decided that Epimetheus would distribute the gifts and Prometheus would act as overseer. What this actually meant is that Epimetheus would do all the work and Prometheus would watch. Initially things went very well, but I suspect that Prometheus fell asleep or wandered off. Epimetheus got bored. He started getting rather free with the limited supply of gifts. What better way to make the task go by quicker? When it came time to distribute gifts to humanity, there was nothing left. This left both brothers both in a major bind, for Zeus would not be pleased.

Around this time Prometheus was summoned to a feast by Zeus. He wanted to check on the gift distribution. Doing so over a meal, then as now, is the best way to check on their progress without being too obvious about it. Prometheus wasn't ready to face the king of the gods over his dereliction of duty, so he came up with a plan of distraction.

Prometheus brought in a beautiful white bull as an offering to Zeus. After his king acknowledged the gift with a seemingly casual wave of his hand, Prometheus realized that the gift alone wasn't enough of a distraction. After the presentation, he butchered the offering, creating two piles from it. One pile was all the best and most useful parts of the animal, covered in the skin and topped with the stomach which is a rather undesirable part, as you well know. The other pile was the bones, draped in fat. Then Prometheus launched into a long meandering speech that went on and on until Zeus and the other guests had plainly lost track. They were just letting it roll over them, waiting with growing impatience for it to end, murmuring among themselves. So finally Prometheus ended his speech and waited for Zeus' response expectantly.

"Say again?" Zeus asked.

"Choose a pile, my lord."

Zeus had no idea what was going on and instead of admitting his impatient inattention, he quickly chose a pile that looked good without being aware of the whys.

"That one," he pointed to the second pile. "I choose that one."

Prometheus chuckled, which was Zeus' first clue that something was afoot. The dining hall became ominously quiet.

"You are so kind and generous to the mortals, oh gracious king," said Prometheus. "By choosing this pile, you have agreed that the offerings the mortals burn in our honor will be the parts that are of no use to them. The rest they will keep for themselves, to feed their families as they praise your generous nature."

Zeus was furious at the gambit played by Prometheus. In his fury, Zeus decreed that mortals would never have the gift of fire needed for light, warmth, cooking, or offerings.

This he had no right to do. The hearth fire is *mine* and all homes are *mine,* whether mortal or divine. By refusing them the use of fire, he essentially banned *me* from my own sacred space.

V. Epimetheus

Prometheus went into hiding, waiting for our king's temper to cool. Epimetheus was not unaware of the trouble they both were in. He arrived late to apologize for mishandling his distribution duty. When Zeus understood what Epimetheus was babbling about, he banished the bungling deity to the surface, to live among the mortals so that he had to toil as they toiled. In comparison to current times, mankind had it easy. No illness, no evil, no misery. Just joy, love, and laughter.

When Prometheus found out about Epimetheus' punishment, he was worried that it was too easy, too light. He sent his brother a message warning him not to accept any gift from Zeus. He figured any gift sent would be more punishment than anything else. Prometheus was, of course, correct. Zeus did have further punishment in mind for Epimetheus' failure. He devised a housewarming gift, and like all gifts from the gods, it bore a price.

The gift was an indestructible jar made by Hephaistos and beautifully decorated by Athene.

Zeus filled that jar with blessings and curses. He filled it so full that even he, the mightiest of the gods, had a hard time putting the lid onto the jar. Yet because of Hephaistos' glorious design, it would open with just a touch and could not come open on its own, no matter the pressure exerted by the contents. Hermes delivered the jar to Epimetheus and told him that it was pandora, the all-gift, and to never open it. Never, ever, open it. No. Matter. What.

Yet there was only one thing Epimetheus could think of when he saw the beautiful jar. All he could think of was showing it off to his mortal neighbors and proclaiming that it was a gift from the king of the gods. By evening, all Epimetheus could think about was the contents of the jar. What is in it? Gold? Jewels? Is it like Amalthea's horn, providing an endless supply of food? Still, surprisingly enough, he resisted the temptation to open it, remembering his brother's warning.

The next day, his mortal neighbors pestered him. "Sure it is a lovely jar, but it is the contents that are important. Surely you misunderstood the directions. Take a look! What is in it, Epimetheus?! As nice as the outside, the inside must be better!"

Their curiosity battered at him like the wind blowing a loose shutter against a house. Still he resisted opening the jar. Then night fell. Epimetheus stared at the jar. Once it moved around a bit due to the energetic contents shifting about.

This was the final straw for Epimetheus. "What if it is a beautiful woman in there?" he murmured.

With that thought, he could no longer resist the temptation to open the jar. Epimetheus lightly touched the lid, thinking he would just peek inside. His gentle touch caused the lid to fly off and shatter as it landed on the floor. Out of the jar poured a gray mist that gradually separated into light and dark. The more he looked, the more distinct the figures within the light and dark areas. These figures swirled around each other, doing battle. Slowly the dark appeared to be overwhelming the light with sheer viciousness. Then, a note sounded and the light retreated out his window and up into the heavens. The dark spread out into the country side with lots of howls and jeering.

Horrified, Epimetheus stared at the jar, realizing he should have left the jar alone. Then he noticed something struggling to get out of the jar. A figure of the light, badly crumpled in the filling of the jar, was having a hard time getting out of it.

Upon exiting the jar, the figure asked, "Where have my brethren gone?"

Epimetheus quietly pointed up into the sky.

"Where have the dark ones gone?"

Epimetheus pointed at the land.

The figure sighed and said, "I will stay instead of returning to Olympos. I will be the light in the dark for the mortals. I will be the one that will keep them going until my brethren find the will to return."

"Who are you?!" Epimetheus finally found his tongue to ask.

"I am Elpis. Though small and frayed, I am the hope that will keep man from completely collapsing upon itself. May the gods forgive your actions and return my brethren to assist in this effort."

Then the figure flew into the countryside.

From that day on, mankind, who had always had a good life, experienced evil. They now live with greed, lies, theft, gluttony, illness, and corruption, all thanks to Epimetheus and his curiosity. There is only hope to get mortals through until the other light figures return. And return they do, but only for short stays, and never in a predictable fashion. Hope is the beacon for all.

As a reminder to Epimetheus of his transgressions, his pretty jar was turned into a woman, named Pandora, and made his wife. She is an empty-headed creature, unworthy of the name woman, I tell you. Good for nothing, but sitting there and looking pretty. A pretty, lifelong punishment for the god of afterthought.

VI. The Theft

All of these events I had from Prometheus, who told me when he snuck into my temple for a visit. Since Zeus took fire away from the mortals, I had no way to see what was happening. I welcomed a visit from my old suitor precisely because he was entertaining and a great way to distract me from my anger.

After he told me the tale of Pandora, I started to pace. The more I paced, the angrier I got, the warmer the stone floor became from the flame of my anger. The angrier I grew the more I paced. I roared my frustration while Prometheus stared at me with large eyes.

"Something has got to be done!" I exclaimed. "Zeus has no right to take me away from the mortals. Their hearth is *mine*, their homes around it were built by *my* design, and he has taken all of that from me. He *gave* that to me!"

I turned when I heard a yelp, to see Prometheus batting at his clothing which I had inadvertently set afire. I apologized and fetched him a belated drink of hospitality. When I returned I was somewhat calmer, though the anger was only banked, not put out.

"I have a suggestion, a solution, but it will mean transgressing against Zeus," he hesitantly stated.

"Out with it. What is your idea?" I demanded.

"I agree that Zeus went too far, punishing you for my own transgression. I will make it right, and because of your value to both mortals and immortals, I will keep your role silent. Give me a bit of your flame and I will carry it down to the mortals, returning that which I caused to be removed from them."

"But Zeus decreed! You'll be punished, and me along with you!"

"No. He will never know it came from you. When questioned, I will claim to have stolen it from Athene's forge or maybe Hephaistos'. You will never be brought into this, and I will repair the breach I have caused you and the damage I caused the mortals."

I sat stunned and thought about it. Part of me hated the idea. I wanted to outright rebel and burn my mark into Zeus' hide. Subtlety isn't my strong suit. This was more practical, but still I worried.

"Zeus will find out and your punishment will be severe. Are you sure you want to do this?"

"Yes. I owe it to you and to the mortals who were punished for my transgressions. I only ask that when the time is right, you send someone to aid me."

I quietly bobbed my head in ascent, surprised at the whole proposal. Prometheus then reached behind him and grabbed a hollow ferula stalk which I had not seen him bring in. He held it out to me and I saw that he had prepared the hollow for fire. I touched the tinder he had placed there and set it to a slow burn. He then closed up the stalk, bowed, and left without another word.

VII. The Offer

"I come to my reason for my visit."

"You want me to rescue Prometheus from his rock and Zeus' eagle?" Herakles stated in a dead voice, glaring at Hestia, fists clenched.

"You are aware of his punishment. Yes I do, but not for free and I am not commanding, but asking. Ask Prometheus where and how to find the apple. And above all keep my part in this silent as he has done these many years. Finding someone to accomplish his release has been my duty in repayment for him returning my fire to you mortals."

The man at her feet appeared ready to argue, or deny her request.

"This is something that can only be done by a willing hero. He will know where to find your apple, and how best to accomplish the difficult task of getting it. While Prometheus can be sneaky, I imagine he tires of his predicament. If you are worried about being tricked, do not set your uncle free until after you have accomplished your task. This may or may not change how he answers your request, however."

Herakles appeared to be thinking over what she said, but still seemed resistant to the idea.

"I have no other advice on how you may accomplish your task without his help. Prometheus is old and wily. He has always been able to accomplish what he set his mind to doing. He will know how to help you to accomplish this labor."

"Very well, my lady. I will do as you advise. I will seek him out and if he helps me find that damned apple, I will set him free of that liver-devouring eagle." Herakles rolled to his hands and knees, wearily climbing to his feet.

When he turned back to his aunt, she was nowhere to be seen. There is only a map burned into the stump where she had sat, displaying the route to where Prometheus was bound. Herakles studied the map carefully before he placed the stump in his fire.

"I will keep your secret, dear aunt. Thank you for the tale, and the guidance."

Forever My Own

by Gerri Leen

Celebrated
For my chastity
Loved
For my purity
Welcomed
For my warmth

Misunderstood, for ages
Zeus, the "wise" one
My baby brother
And the oldest of us, vomited out first
Knowing all the while that
I am the true eldest

He watched me warily
As we worked out our places
Olympus only big enough for one king
And a consort, not a true queen
Would Zeus have swallowed me?
If I had not outsmarted him?

Poseidon wanted me
His great watery skin
Smelling of seaweed and salt
I am fire
What life would I have in the ocean?

Of course I said no

Apollo wanted me
Light-bringer, singer of songs
He would have drowned out
My crackle
Outshone my light
Fire disappears against the sun

I begged Zeus to let me remain untouched
He was moved
By relief as much as anything
"You shall have first share,"
And the freedom to do
As I will, owned only by myself

I hid my smile
I bowed my head and gave thanks
For giving me what I was due
For failing to see
I would outlive them all
Fire never dies, not for long anyway

Queen of Hearth and Home I

by Kathy Mac

She clawed her way back to university in her forties
after nursing to their deaths
first her father, so treasured she bought him
    spanking porn,
then her neo-Victorian mother who saw her as a
    mass of obligations
and their disavowals.

Houseplants thrive in her choc-a-bloc apartment,
    feng-shui stumped by the
desk, piano, jukebox – raffle-won behemoth – and
    disguised liquor cabinet, all
barnacled in three lives' detritus. Almost every book
    she's ever read. Dust
and cat hair worn to a felt carpet.

For years she neglected the boxes of dirt hung on
    the balcony rail. Still they're green,
with moss, a few rash perennials, and sprouts from
    seeds shat by the nesting pigeons
she rousts each morn and night, aided by her twin
    feral cats, Thought and Memory.
Rescues, dwarfed by a rough early life.

The Sacred Fire

by David W. Landrum

A bride, Dianthe thought as she lay down to sleep that night, *should not be sad.* Of course, sadness always came. Girls cried at weddings. Leaving your home, your mother and sisters, father and brothers, the familiarity of the house in which you grew up, and your friends brought sorrow. Tears at weddings, however, always were erased by joy. Love, a future that included children, the mysteries of the marriage bed, enfranchisement as a full member of the community — all these things elided the sadness of the passage into womanhood. They did not ease the pain Dianthe felt. She cried silently, not wanting her mother to hear; or her younger sister with whom she shared a bed.

She wept because she did not want to be married. She had hoped to be the girl who would succeed Phaedra as the priestess of Hestia.

Phaedra's home looked like most every other house in their rather substantial settlement (the men talked about obtaining status as a city). Made of brick, with a red tile roof, a garden out back, it spread beyond the garden to include a small shed housing a milk cow and a few chickens that pecked for insects in a tiny meadow farther out (where the cow went out at certain times of the day to graze). Adjacent to the house sat the temple of Hestia.

The temple did not dazzle visitors. A simple round building with a domed roof, flowers planted all around it, sheltered by two white birch trees, it sat next to Phaedra's place. A small cloistered walkway joined the two buildings. Inside the round structure, an image of the goddess Hestia looked down on the sacred fire that burned there continually.

The townspeople considered no spot more sacred than Hestia's fire. It had burned perpetually since the founding of the town a hundred years ago. Only once had it gone out. The priestess tended it and fed tiny sticks of wood to keep the small blaze burning.

Dianthe shifted, trying to get more comfortable. Kora, her sister, stirred and said something in her sleep. Dianthe lay still, not wanting to wake her. Her mind raced on.

She thought of Phaedra, beautiful in every way a woman could be beautiful. Slender, pretty, she had quietly gone about the task of being priestess, serving with gentle energy and grace and purpose. Being a priestess of Hestia demanded much of a woman. You had to stay up all night, every night, and tend the fire. It must never go out. If a priestess ever let the fire go out, obligation demanded she take her own life as atonement for her failure, as letting the fire go out constituted blasphemy. The old women said the priestess two in the succession back from Phaedra had let the fire die. She had hanged herself the next day. The village consecrated a woman to be the new priestess and had fire brought from the sacred hearth in the capital to begin worship once again.

It would be a fearful thing to be priestess, Dianthe thought, lying in the quiet dark of her home. Still, her soul filled with bitterness because she had wanted this more than anything else and it had been denied her. By tomorrow night she would be a wife and would leave maidenhood. Hestia's priestesses were required to be virgins.

Dianthe was eight years old when she first met Phaedra. The village assigned girls to do the morning chores at the priestess' home while she slept. The priestess slept four hours, which was the maximum time the fire could be left unattended. It was the only time she was permitted to rest unless she had an acolyte, and Phaedra was not yet at the age when she would be training girls to take over her duties. The village elders would appointed seven acolytes when the priestess turned fifty. That would be in a few years, but Dianthe calculated and knew she would be the right age then to take over the ministry of the sacred fire.

Dianthe liked Phaedra and thought her beautiful, but she also loved the way she showed kindness to everyone. She smiled, never spoke harshly, and never scolded when the girls made mistakes or broke things on the farm. Even when the girl who worked for her did something inappropriate, she did not seize her by the hair or the ear, shake, slap, or sternly rebuke her. She simply talked to the girl about why her behavior was improper, how it dishonored the goddess, and how it fell short of the propriety a maiden should always display. Her words had their effect; more than if she had been harsh. The two times Dianthe misbehaved and Phaedra spoke to her, the girl dissolved in tears of shame; it took a week for her to recover from the priestess' mild, kind, thoughtful rebuke. She never again misbehaved in the temple after the second time. Phaedra did not remind her of her failings, as others often did, keeping lists in their heads and enumerating her sins when she did something wrong.

Before the selection, Dianthe would go to the priestess' house to do chores twice a week. She milked Phaedra's cow, fed her chickens, gathered eggs, and pulled weeds in the flower bed around the temple. Then she returned to home to help with breakfast and the morning baking. The village supplied the priestess with food, so she did not have to spend time cooking. Dianthe would bring her bread, sometimes fruit and olives. She would be awake and cheerful, and would kiss Dianthe and speak pleasantly with her. Even though Dianthe had already had breakfast, she would sometimes drink wine or eat a few olives as the priestess had her breakfast and answered her questions.

"Do you like being a priestess?" she asked.

The smile Dianthe loved so much would come to Phaedra's lips. "It's a joy beyond description, Dianthe, a complete joy."

"Did you ever want to be married?"

"Well, I never had that option. I was chosen to be an acolyte at six and consecrated as a priestess when I was thirteen."

"Mother says it's a pity such a beautiful woman as you never had a chance to marry, and has to live her whole life as a virgin."

Phaedra laughed, almost merrily. "I don't think of myself as someone to be pitied. I have lived a happy life. One does not need to be married to be happy."

"What gives you happiness?"

"The goddess gives me joy. I live a quiet life. I serve our village and cherish the people here. All of these things are my reward and the source of my happiness, as is my closeness to the goddess herself."

As Dianthe walked home one morning in fall when the fields showed a good harvest, she knew she wanted to be a priestess of Hestia. She told her mother as much.

* * *

Her family consisted of her mother and father, three boys, and two girls. Their father rejoiced to have strong sons who could work the land with him. He saw their two daughters as a means to make alliances with other clans in the area; especially by marrying off Dianthe, who was beautiful.

"But we don't want to anger the goddess," her mother said after she told him about Dianthe's desire to serve the altar rather than to marry.

Their family did not tend toward religiosity. Still, they shared the piety that marked most everyone in their settlement. You did not offend the gods. Refusing to consider a daughter for service might constitute hubris. Her father had increased their family wealth by hard work and good management; had bought two poorly-run farms, made them productive, and received rent from the former owners, who now lived as his tenants; he served on the city council; he hobnobbed with the wealthy, who seemed to like him. One of them, Clonius, had a son Dianthe's age and said he thought her "a beautiful young woman." She could see the shape of her future in this; it was not the future she desired.

She went to Phaedra and told her.

"Why do you wish to serve Hestia?" she asked.

"Because—" She wanted to say it was because she loved Phaedra so much, admired everything about her, and wanted to be like her, but she hesitated.

"You must tell me the truth, Dianthe."

She blushed but obeyed the priestess' admonition.

"I want to serve the goddess because you represent her; you're so kind and good, and so pure. I want to be like you are, lady priestess. I want to be kind and pure."

Phaedra smiled. "Your words show me you are already those things. But I don't decide who will be the next priestess. The council does, though they consult with me on the choice. You've served well, and I think you are indeed a kind, devout, thoughtful young maiden. I will give them your name for an acolyte, a girl who may possibly become priestess. I pick seven, and all of you serve at different times. Much of what you do will be no different from the way you have helped me out over the years, but you will also assist me in some of the duties of my office. As great as your desire to serve Hestia may be, this is not, I'm afraid, much of a consideration in the way priestesses are chosen."

"If I am not chosen here, could I serve at another temple?"

Phaedra laughed and took Dianthe's hands. "Child, there are no other temples of Hestia — well, I shouldn't say that — but there are none I know of or have heard of. We are an oddity because we do have a temple dedicated to the goddess and maintain a priestess. No other towns or cities I've seen do and many, indeed most, believe Hestia is worshipped in the home and should not have a temple."

"Why not?"

"She is the goddess of the hearth, of family, and of life, the lives we all live within the sacredness of our homes. As such, Hestia already has an altar: the hearth in your own home. She has a sacred space: your house. She has priestesses: your mother, your sister, and you. Seeing the goddess in this way is very important. It is important for our people to think of her in this manner because it tells us day-to-day things we do in our homes are sacred, as sacred as a what is done in a temple. We have a temple and it will continue as a place of worship. But I can see the point of those who think there should be no temples of Hestia. I'll recommend you for an acolyte. I have to do that soon."

"Why, lady priestess?" Phaedra did not look like she was fifty.

"Time is running out."

Dianthe's eyes filled with alarm. "Running out? What do you mean, lady priestess?"

"I'm not well, Dianthe. I think my days are numbered. Someone will need to take up the office, and very soon."

In the spring of next year, Phaedra would die of cancer at age forty-four. She reviewed the acolytes in the next seven months.

Dianthe and the others six girls did the chores all of them had done previously. They milked, fed the chickens, weeded, cleaned her house, and did her laundry. But they also learned the proper way to feed the sacred fire, carry off the ashes; and they learned the simple prayers said throughout the day before the image of Hestia. Dianthe worked diligently. She memorized the prayers, paid close attention so as to master procedures for keeping the sacred fire burning, and worked with all her heart as Phaedra grew more and more ill. Her hair turned grey. She began to lose weight and grow feeble. It tortured Dianthe's heart to see her decline. She devoted herself to her tasks, hoping she would have the honor of becoming priestess of the goddess of hearth and family.

Dianthe possessed a perceptive mind, and even as she bent her soul to the task of being competent at the lore and tasks of the temple, she noticed how her father looked at her and saw when she carded wool or weeded the family garden. The stern resolution in his face and the look in his eyes told her he wanted her married. Finally he told her the match had been arranged.

"You're such a lucky girl," her friend said. "Isodemos' father has all the money in the world. You'll live in a fine house and never be in want."

But Dianthe felt her spirit wither like a flower when the weather grows cold. She wanted to go to Phaedra, but the priestess was too ill to do anything but see to her duties at the fire. When winter arrived, a woman of forty or so came to assist Phaedra, who by now could barely get around and was in a great deal of pain. The woman they chose to assist her was not a priestess of Hestia but had taken a vow of chastity and had served as a temple maiden at the shrine to Athena at Pylos when she was young. Phaedra died just as winter broke and the cold, uncertain weather of early spring began. The woman who had helped her in her last days, Tryphosa, agreed to stay and perform the duties until the new priestess was named.

    Surely, Dianthe thought as the weather warmed and the fields and forest around the town show green once more, Phaedra would have mentioned me. Surely she saw how much I wanted to serve and how I gave myself so fully to learning the things a priestess must know how to do. She remembered the sadness of Phaedra's funeral. It had not rained, but the day arrived overcast and windy. A cold breeze blew in from the sea. Since Phaedra had lived a life of chastity and was consecrated to Hestia, men could not touch her corpse; neither could any woman who had known a man. The acolytes washed her, wrapped her body, and carried it to a space in a grove of willows, lowered the body into a grave, and covered it with earth and then with flowers. People wept and mourned; men and women. Phaedra had been an exemplary woman; pure, holy, without reproach. At home, Dianthe wept inconsolably. Even when grief mastered her, she wondered if she would be the priestess or not. If

Phaedra had recommended her, she thought, her father would have relent and break the engagement. Dianthe fervently hoped it would be so.

At dark on the night of the funeral, when her grief abated, her mother gave her porridge to eat and a cup of wine to drink. As she ate, her father sat down beside her.

"Do you feel better, child?"

"Yes, Father."

"We all miss Phaedra. She was a living picture of holiness and devotion. I know you hoped to take her office, daughter. That will not be. The council has chosen someone else. I'm sorry. I truly am. I know it is a disappointment, but the goddess has made her will clear. She has decided another will serve her."

By that time, Dianthe had cried out all he tears. She felt only a dull, sorrowful disappointment. She also knew nothing could reverse what her father had said. She knew she would be married, and probably soon

* * *

Her mother chided her for sulking the next day.

"Hestia is the goddess of hearth and family, and of the home, which is a sacred space. You disgrace her name, sulking like a water rat because you were not chosen to be her priestess. You also do despite to the memory of blessed Phaedra, whose obedience to the goddess served as an example to us all. Shame on you, young maiden. I would take a strap to you if you weren't all but a woman. Now go outside and wait by the well house until I call for you."

Standing by the well house occupied the lowest rung on the family's agenda of punishments. Early morning made it cool. Dew sparkled on the grass and flowers. In some places, wisps of fog hung above the land. The sky arched over her in a deep, cloudless blue.

Fate, the god, the goddess herself perhaps, had killed her prayers and her desire. Her father wanted her married and wanted to ally his family with the family of Colonius, a thing that would be prosperous to everyone in both clans. Her children, she thought, would be privileged. If the village were granted status as a town, they might someday be rulers and judges. Still, the realization that she would not live her life as a virgin dedicated to Hestia's service, that her dream of a quiet, chaste existence had evaporated like water spilled on the paving stones around the well house, hurt her soul. She did not want to acknowledge the wisdom of her mother's admonition, but she had to admit its correctness. When she stepped back from her resentment and disappointment, she knew she could not sulk and pout. Life bristled with difficulties. She needed to be obedient.

Her sister came to fetch her after two hours. She returned to the house, knelt before her mother, and clasped her hands, raising them in supplication, her head bowed to show her sorrow and repentance. "Rise, child." When she stood, her mother embraced her.

* * *

Dianthe felt sleep start to claim her as she lay in bed and remembered. She needed to be joyous. She had a beautiful wedding gown. Clonius had arranged for feasting, dancing, music, and games at the celebration of her marriage. The midwife had examined her and said she would do fine on her first night (she did not have to be cut) and that she would bear children easily. Children were high on the agenda for men like Clonius and her father, and mothers cherished grandchildren. She should not be cynical. Lydia, whom the council had chosen, would be a capable priestess. She was a lot like Phaedra: quiet, kind, thoughtful, obedient.

A good choice, Dianthe thought groggily.

Sleep claimed her as quiet settled on the town, on the grave of Phaedra, on Lydia the new priestess, and on Dianthe, soon to be a bride.

The Bath of Hestia

by P. Sufenas Virius Lupus

No one remembers the pool, the place
where Aktaion took his fatal glance
at Artemis, became a rutting stag,
and was torn apart by his hounds.

No one recalls the river, the reason
that Tiresias stole his final sight
of Athena's virgin body bathing, burning
vision from his eyes into his soul.

But the place and the time when Hestia
was seen bathing by Her nephew
Hephaistos — when He was but a child —
will never be forgotten: the Nile of Egypt.

Newly born of Hera without Zeus' seed,
child Hephaistos was a Phoebus for beauty,
sound in every limb, brilliant in comeliness,
a second Helios, a young bright Phosphoros.

His aunt took Herself to the Nile's source
and submerged Herself, causing the upswell
of the river's yearly inundation —
forever virgin, forever sustaining life.

Child Hephaistos saw Her, innocent,
Her fire setting the waters ablaze, a-boil,
and thinking She would embrace Him as always,
He ran to Her side through the surging tide.

He was burned, boiled, scorched, scathed,
made hideous, monstrous, and Her horrified;
but, He knew the tempering of metals after,
and was regarded as crafting creator in Egypt.

Therefore, lament Hera's beautiful son's loss,
and praise Hephaistos for His skill in all art and
        arms,
not the sadness of His burning in the fiery water;
and sing of Hestia of the rising Nile's tide.

Guess Who's Coming to Dinner: Hestia, Hospitality, and Interstate Relations in Classical Athens

by Nicholas D. Cross

Hestia, the virgin goddess, guardian of the sacred fire, is not often associated with interstate relations. Being a domestic figure, confined to the realm of the home, Hestia may not appear to have any relevance to affairs between city-states. In fact, however, in classical Athens, the goddess of the hearth played a rather significant role in this arena by creating a common identity for those engaged in interstate collaborative endeavors and by providing a deeper level of signification than just political and military cooperation. This can be demonstrated by examining the epilogue to interstate alliance negotiations in Athens, the practice of entertaining foreign ambassadors with a meal of hospitality (*xenia*) at the sacred hearth in the Prytaneion.

If modern scholarship is correct in reducing interstate alliances, as well as other forms of interstate activity, to nothing more than pragmatic agreements designed to counteract military emergencies, why did the Athenians take the extra time, an entire day, in the negotiations for a special meal with the representatives of their new allies? Why was it hosted in the Prytaneion, the town hall of the city-state? What was the purpose for all of this, and how did contemporaries perceive it? In order to answer these questions, this paper reexamines the part Hestia played in that meal. After the negotiation process for an alliance, which involved the participation of the whole community and created a sense of domestic unity, all of the diners in the Prytaneion would have recognized in Hestia's presence the symbols of hospitality, helping the wronged and the family unit. Just as the alliance negotiations created a sense of domestic unity, so the closing meal created a sense of interstate unity. In short, the shared meal at the common hearth was celebratory and commemorative, and accentuated the social and religious values upon which Athenian politico-military pacts rested.

By the classical period, the Athenians had entered into interstate alliances for some time and had created general procedures involving the participation of the whole community. Foreign ambassadors seeking an alliance with the Athenians first approached their council (βουλή). If it agreed to their request, the matter was passed on to the assembly (ἐκκλησία), the larger legislative body composed of all eligible citizens, which had the authority to take actions concerning war, peace, and alliances.[1] The assembly meeting opened with a ceremony consisting of a sacrifice, a prayer and a curse, rituals designed to create a psychological sense of solemnity and solidarity, and to give the proposed alliance a greater significance than just a politico-military agreement.² After the foreign ambassadors made their case, extensive debate ensued among the citizens until the proposal was put to a vote; in this way, through the voice of the people, the alliance received legitimacy. Constructing an alliance, therefore, was not achieved by dictate but through public debate. It was larger than one individual or political faction; it was a communal achievement. The final act for the assembly was to write up the specific provisions into a decree (ψήφισμα), and to commission a stone copy (στήλη) for permanent display in the sacred precinct on the Acropolis.

But there was important work remaining. Chosen representatives participated in a ceremony consisting of a sacrifice and the swearing of an oath, rituals that invoked divine protection, but also accentuated the social signification of the alliance. With the gods as witnesses, the swearing of oaths, which reiterated the shared political and military goals of the alliance, over the head of a sacrificial animal, brought the participants even closer together. These performative aspects reinforced the common interests of the two parties and provided "metaphors of unity."³ The discourse and the drama of the opening ceremonies were instrumental in transforming what had begun as a domestic communal activity into an interstate communal activity.

There was yet another practice that continued this transformative feature of the alliance process. From at least the mid-fifth century BCE, the Athenian assembly generally made provision in the final treaty,

"to invite the ambassadors [of the new ally] for a meal of hospitality in the Prytaneion on the next day."
καλέσαι τὴν πρεσβείαν τὴν τῶν [xxx] ἐπὶ ξένια ἐς τὸ πρυτανεῖον ἐς αὔριον.

Of the eighty-five times that this invitation appears in inscriptions from classical Athens, about a dozen are for foreign ambassadors who negotiated an alliance.[4] But since many inscriptions are fragmentary and the extant corpus is by no means complete, there are surely many more examples lost to history. Indeed, Demosthenes says that in his time this invitation was customary (τὸ νόμιμον ἔθος).[5] Why, then, did this become a general feature of the procedural conduct of Athenian interstate relations? Why did it take place in the Prytaneion? What does all of this say about the cognitive framework of Athenian alliances? Questions such as these can be addressed by taking a closer look at the role of Hestia in the meal and in interstate relations.

Having a meal around a hearth was an old cult tradition extending back at least to Mycenaean times, when the hearth was situated within a king's palace (*megaron*). Even at this time, as Katherine Harrell and Rachel Fox have recently shown, such meals were instrumental for the king to create alliances with the guests.[6] Although in this way the palatial hearth acted as the center of political life, it also contained a highly charged religious significance. Arguing against a view that divorces the political from the religious aspects of this activity, James Wright demonstrates how closely attached the Mycenaean kings were to the maintenance of the hearth as a cult institution. The political head was intimately involved in sacrifices and libations and in the preservation of the fire. Although the king as the head of a "hearth-wanax cult" eventually disappeared from Greek civilization, replaced by the city-state as the custodian of a civic hearth in the Prytaneion, the communal meal with foreign guests continued to endure.[7]

In the classical period, when foreign ambassadors entered the Prytaneion, they would see the eternal flame of the hearth, which, of course, is another way of referring to the goddess Hestia. Although she does not appear often in the literary record, she was of great importance to the Greeks nonetheless. Hesiod records that she is the first born child of Kronos and Rhea.[8] The *Homeric Hymn to Aphrodite* tells how she rejected the marriage proposals from both Poseidon and Apollo:

"She, the splendid one of the gods, was very much unwilling and firmly refused. But, touching the head of father Zeus, the aegis-bearer, she swore a great oath, which has been fulfilled, that she would be a virgin all her days. So father Zeus gave to her a good honor instead of marriage, and she sits within the house, holding the best portion. In all the temples of the gods she receives honor, and among all mortals she is chief of the gods."[9]

In other words, she became, in the words of this anthology's title, "first and last." The *Homeric Hymn to Hestia*, for example, praises her as one without whom "mortals hold no banquet, where one does not duly pour sweet wine in offering to Hestia both first and last."[10] Although ubiquitous in this sense, she was rarely represented visually and no cult images of her have been found in Athens from the classical period. However, this might be, as Stephen Miller suggests, because "the hearth alone may have provided an adequate symbol of Hestia's presence."[11] She was first and last, inconspicuous yet always present in the sacred fire.

Her overall significance is striking, for, as the Hymn to Aphrodite says, she was a virgin goddess who dwelt at the common hearth in the Prytaneion as well as the hearths of private homes. Prima facie, her domestic seclusion is not a characteristic associated with interstate relations. In modern parlance she appears to be more of a symbol for isolationism than internationalism. On the contrary, however, a close look at Hestia's symbolism in the traditions of welcoming strangers (*xenia*), helping the wronged, and integrating the family shows how her presence accentuated the sociocultural features of interstate activity.

The terminology for the meal presented to the foreign ambassadors – *xenia* – was distinctive. Other meals offered in the Prytaneion, deipnon or sitesis, were generally for Athenian citizens – athletes, traders, benefactors, and citizen ambassadors.[12] *Xenia*, however, was reserved for outsiders. This has a long tradition in ancient Greece: Homer's elite heroes regularly extended *xenia* to old as well as new friends. At a time when hostels and inns did not exist, it was an obligatory service for a host to offer *xenia* to strangers and travelers.[13] By the classical age, however, as mentioned above, the city-state had assumed this role of host. This is one reason why the *xenia* for the ambassadors took place in the Prytaneion. Besides the fact that the building had the facilities to host a large meal, the Prytaneion, with the eternal flame of the hearth, was a symbol of the city-state. The meal was not between individuals but between two communities. "The state's adoption of hospitality," writes Sarah Bolmarcich, "is another way to create friendship between states via the ambassadors negotiating the treaties in question."[14] In all of this stood the presence of Hestia. Pindar, in fact, expressly links Hestia, "first of gods," to acts of hospitality.[15] And the verbal form of Hestia (ἑστιᾶν) means "to receive at one's hearth, to entertain, to feast." The goddess of the home accentuated the sociocultural features of *xenia*.

Xenia is also associated with refuge for those in need. Since the acts of hospitality were offered to strangers, the recipients of this generosity were often exiles, refugees, and other undesirables in their home city-state. "*Xenia* is a species of asylum," writes Robert Garland, "that may well have developed out of the same impulse to provide protection for those who were unprotected."[16] This is significant to the present discussion because the hearth was the traditional place of refuge for suppliants in ancient Greece. For example, when weary Odysseus arrived at the island of Scheria, he clasped the knees of Queen Arete in supplication and then sat beside the hearth of the megaron until King Alcinous received him and entertained him with a feast.[17] In the fifth century BCE, the Athenian Themistocles, a fugitive after the Persian Wars, fled to Molossia. Queen Phthia received him favorably and instructed him to sit by the hearth, "the most solemn kind of supplication." She also entrusted him with her infant son, perhaps associating the exile with the most innocent member of the royal family. At the hearth Themistocles was in a position that was "most sacred, and ... not to be refused," so the king accepted him and protected him from his enemies.[18] "The suppliant," writes F.S. Naiden on these and other examples of petitioners at a hearth, "has combined an approach to the hearth, and approach to the king, and access to the king's family."[19] The hearth environment reminded all of the responsibilities to help those in genuine need and to integrate them into the community.

That vulnerable condition, the status of a refugee, was, in effect, the same for the city-state petitioning the Athenians for an alliance. All involved at the meal in the Prytaneion would have reflected on the normative responsibility to come to the assistance of the weak and the wronged. Since the conduct of interstate relations was a personal activity, the Greeks took moral considerations into account much more seriously than modern states do. It is easy, therefore, for scholars today — classicists, ancient historians, and political scientists — to dismiss the possibility of these factors serving as genuine motivations for interstate behavior, preferring to view them as propaganda or, worse, as jiggery-pokery, like the modern promotion of democratic ideals as a justification for interventionism. It is difficult, however, to dismiss the frequent appearance in the ancient Athenian accounts of the slogan "helping the wronged" (βοηθεῖν τοῖς ἀδικουμένοις) as an ideal objective for involvement in interstate affairs.[20] Of course, much of this is for rhetorical effect, but the point is that in the articulation of their alliances, the Athenians accentuated the moral obligations. In the same way the hearth, the place of refuge, represented those same considerations.[21]

On a symbolic and even a phenomenological level, the meal between representatives of each city-state, along with the discernible presence of Hestia, was celebratory (of the achieved alliance), commemorative (of the moral responsibilities behind interstate action), and constitutive (of a shared, familial identity). In his famous article comparing Hestia and Hermes, Jean-Pierre Vernant highlighted the symbolic importance of the hearth in terms of integrating strangers into the community. "The hearth, the meal, the food also have the property of opening the domestic circle to those who are not members of the family, of enrolling them in the family community. The suppliant, hunted from his home and wandering abroad crouches at the hearth when he seeks to enter a new group in order to recover the social and religious roots he has lost."[22] In the context of an interstate alliance, the negotiation process created a transition by which the petitioning city-state moved from the status of an outsider to a friend. Sharing a meal at the place of the hearth, moreover, marked the point at which the friend became family.

John Gould describes the hearth as "emblem of the solidarity of the group with other forms of ritual to incorporate outsiders into the οἶκος."[23] Just as each home had a private hearth, so the one in the Prytaneion, the common hearth, symbolized the corporate body. A scholiast to Thucydides calls the Prytaneion an οἶκος μέγας, the great house of the city-state.[24] The meal with the foreign ambassadors was set, as it were, within the house of the city-state, at the table of the communal family, which now incorporated two city-states. Sharing a meal, an intimate activity, therefore, represented a greater sense of unity. "At a deeper level," writes Susan Sherratt on feasting in epic, "feasting can be said to encapsulate values that are likely to have simultaneously created and confirmed a collective ideology: the values of companionship and commensality, equal sharing and individual esteem, reciprocity and the obligations of hospitality."[25] The practice symbolized the virtual extended family status that the two allies now shared on account of their political accord.

Finally, at some point after the meal the foreign ambassadors returned home, accompanied by Athenian representatives who would participate in a correlating ceremony of oaths, sacrifices, and perhaps another shared meal. Later, the two parties went even further and commemorated the alliance with more sacrifices and processions.[26] Isocrates mentions the custom (ἔθος) of holding festivals after the conclusion of interstate agreements, in which the city-states offered common prayers and sacrifices. By celebrating in this manner, Isocrates continues, "we are reminded of the kinship which originated among us, are disposed to be more kindly towards each other in the future and to renew our old friendships and to make new ones."[27] The celebrations connected the past and the present, commemorating the long-standing relationships and encouraging the creation of new ones to perpetuate the interstate ties.

This paper concentrated on the part which Hestia played in Athenian interstate relations. The whole process of constructing an alliance — from the initial proposal to the concluding meal in the Prytaneion — was a communal activity with highly charged social connotations on a domestic and an interstate level. Sharing a meal around the hearth created a reflective environment in which the participants contemplated the tradition of *xenia*, the normative obligation to help the wronged, and the integration of the two city-states into a virtual family. Because of the influence of the unwedded goddess of hearth and home, these features gave a greater sense of purpose to the political and military objectives, built up the conceptual framework of the parties in alliance, and activated a sense of solidarity.

Notes
1) Aristot. *Pol*. 4.1298a.
2) Aeschin. 1.23; Dem. 19.70; Din. 2.14, 16.
3) Steiner 1994, 61-99.
4) Those that have a certain connection to foreign ambassadors involved in an alliance: *IG* I (3) 11 (Segesta), 123 (Carthage), *IG* II (2) 17 (Thasos), 21 (Seuthes), 22 (Amadocus), 24 (Thasos), 34 (Chios), 40 (Thebes), 41 (Byzantium), 116 (Thessalian League), 127 (northern kings), 175 (Thessalian League).
5) Dem. 19.234.
6) Harrell and Fox 2008, 28-37. Hestia's connection to politics: Kajava 2004, 1-20.
7) Wright 1994, 57-60. The Prytaneion building and its location: Miller 1978; Schmalz 2006, 33-81.
8) Hes. *Theog*. 453.
9) Hom. *Hymn Aph*. 5.22-33.
10) Hom. *Hymn Hest*. 29 (cf. 24).
11) Miller 1978, 15.
12) Cinalli 2015, 35-40.
13) Finley 1978, 46-108; Herman 1987.
14) Bolmarcich 2010, 124.
15) Pind. Nem. 11.1-3.
16) Garland 2014, 129.
17) Hom. *Od*. 7.142-232
18) Plut. *Them*. 24.2-3; cf. Thuc 1.136.2-137.1; Diod. Sic. 11.56.1-4; Nep. *Them*. 8.4.
19) Naiden 2006, 38; cf. 98-99.

20) "Helping the wronged and alliances: Andoc. 3.13; Isoc. 4.53, 8.28-30, 139; 14.1; Dem. 16.14-15; 18.96-100, 177-178; IG II 2 112.32-34.

21) Contrasting views of helping the wronged Low 2007, 175-211; Hunt 2010, 95-97; Christ 2012, 118-176. It was in the Prytaneion that the orphans of those who had died under the Thirty Tyrants were provided with an obol of sustenance (Miller 1978, 11-12).

22) Vernant 1969, 146-147.

23) Gould 1973, 97.

24) Schol. Thuc. 2.15.2.

25) Sheratt 2004, 308.

26) E.g. IG II 2 112.10-11; Dem. 18.215-218.

27) Isoc. 4.43.

Bibliography

Bolmarcich, Sarah, 2010. "Communal Values in Ancient Diplomacy and Culture." In Ralph M. Rosen and Ineke Sluiter, eds. *Valuing Others in Classical Antiquity*. 113-136. Leiden: Brill.

Christ, Matthew. 2012. *The Limits of Altruism in Democratic Athens*. Cambridge: Cambridge University Press.

Cinalli, Agela. 2015. Τὰ ξένια: *La cerimonia di ospitalità cittadina*. Roma: Sapienza Università Editrice.

Finley, Moses I. 1978. *The World of Odysseus*. 2nd edition. New York: The Viking Press.

Garland, Robert. 2014. *Wandering Greeks: The Ancient Greek Diaspora from the Age of Homer to the Death of Alexander the Great*. Princeton: Princeton University Press.

Gould, John. 1973. "Hiketeia." *Journal of Hellenic Studies* 93: 74-103.

Harrell, Katherine and Rachel Fox. 2008. "An Invitation to War: Constructing Alliances and Allegiances through Mycenaean Palatial Feasts." In Sera Baker et al., eds. *Food and Drink in Archaeology*. Volume 1. 28-37. Totnes: Prospect Books.

Herman, Gabriel. 1987. *Ritualised Friendships and the Greek City*. Cambridge: Cambridge University Press.

Hunt, Peter. 2010. *War, Peace, and Alliance in Demosthenes' Athens*. New York: Cambridge University Press.

Kajava, Mika. 2004. "Hestia Hearth, Goddess, and Cult." *Harvard Studies in Classical Philology* 102: 1-20.

Low, Polly. 2007. *Interstate Relations in Classical Greece: Morality and Power*. Cambridge: Cambridge University Press.

Miller, Stephen. 1978. *The Prytaneion: Its Function and Architectural Form*. Berkeley: University of California Press.

Naiden, Fred S. 2006. *Ancient Supplication*. Oxford: Oxford University Press.

Schmalz, Geoffrey C. R. 2006. "The Athenian Prytaneion Discovered?" *Hesperia* 75: 33-81.

Sheratt, Susan. 2004. "Feasting in Homeric Epic." In James Wright, ed. *The Mycenaean Feast*. 301-337. Princeton: The American School of Classical Studies at Athens.

Steiner, Deborah. 1994. *The Tyrant's Writ: Myths and Images of Writing in Ancient Greece*. Princeton: Princeton University Press.

Vernant, Jean Pierre. 1969. "Hestia-Hermes: The Religious Expression of Space and Movement among the Greeks." *Social Science Information* 8: 131-168.

Wright, James C. 1994. "The Spatial Configuration of Belief: The Archaeology of Mycenaean Religion." In Susan Alcock and Robin Osborne, eds. *Placing the Gods: Sanctuaries and Sacred Space in Ancient Greece*. 37-78. Oxford: Clarendon Press.

Hestia of the Campfire

by Lyssa Little Bear

It is in the blaze of the campfire,
the crackle and hiss of the flames,
that I feel your presence, great goddess of the fire.
Hestia, goddess of the hearth fire, I call out to you
as we gather around the flames,
sharing stories, sharing tales, sharing our lives.
We come together, O Hestia, as our ancestors did,
to cook, to talk, to laugh, to love,
all in the glow of your warmth.

Prayer For a Peaceful Home

by Amanda Artemisia Forrester

Fair Eirene, Goddess of peace
Spread your feathered wings over my home.
Gentle Hestia of the flame, who dwells in the hearth
Let us remember the value of family.
Let only words of love be spoken here
Let harmony reign in this house
And the hearts of those who dwell within.
Eirene, Hestia, sweet Goddesses
May you both feel welcome in my home.

Gluten-Free Italian Spaghetti Meatballs
by Alexeigynaix

This is an adaptation of a recipe from my mother's mother's family. Proportions for the herbs and spices are not provided because people's tastes differ and the adaptation is a work in progress anyway. (The original recipe features Accent, you see; Accent, otherwise known as monosodium glutamate, is not friendly to people on gluten-free diets.) In order to test flavor proportions, take an about-meatball-sized chunk of the ground beef mixture, microwave it just long enough to cook it through, and taste, then add herbs and spices as necessary. This will not quite convey the flavor of the meatballs after an hour or two simmering in tomato sauce with bay leaves, though.

My divination confirms that the labor and the first and last portions of the results of this recipe are an appropriate offering to Hestia. I relate this recipe to her because the original version tastes like home to me. I am not gluten-free myself, but I have family members who are, and I make this recipe to welcome them into my home for a shared meal.

Ingredients:
2-3 medium onions
1-2 cups gluten-free bread crumbs
3 lbs ground beef

granulated garlic
oregano
basil
parsley
salt
pepper
24 oz tomato paste (or four six-ounce cans)
72 oz water (or 12 six-ounce canfuls)
bay leaves
olive oil

Instructions:

Chop onions finely; set half aside. Mix bread crumbs, other half of onions, and herbs and spices (excluding bay leaves) into ground beef. Form into meatballs about one inch in diameter.

Add tomato paste, water, and bay leaves to large pot. Stir well.

Heat frying pan. Add olive oil. Brown meatballs in batches, adding them to the sauce pot as they come out of the pan.

Brown the rest of the onions in the same frying pan. Add onions and pan scrapings to the pot.

Simmer uncovered one and a half to two hours. Serve over gluten-free spaghetti, optionally topped with shredded parmesan cheese and accompanied by gluten-free bread (there is an excellent recipe on the King Arthur flour website) and green salad.

Should feed several people, or one person for several days.

To Hestia on Her Birth-Feast

by P. Sufenas Virius Lupus

Goddess Hestia, primordial fire of the hearth,
without Whom "home" cannot be:

may You be born anew on this day for all those
fortunate enough to have a hearth of their own;

may You be born anew now, soon, quickly, quickly,
for those who do not have a hearth at present;

may You shine brightly and guide to Your hearths
those who are without shelter at this time of year;

may Your warmth be kindled in the hearts of all
who honor the Gods, Your kindred and co-equals;

in every spark, in every flame, in every source of
      heat
may You be praised and thanked for Your blessed
      presence.

Khaire Hestia!

Hymn to Hestia
by Jessica Orlando and Peter Ringo

Hymn to Hestia

words Homer/Shelmerdine; music Rachmaninov   arr. Jessica Orlando and Peter Ringo

"Bogoroditse Devo" by Sergei Rachmaninov; set with Homeric Hymn no. 24, "To Hestia" trans. © 1995 Susan C. Shelmerdine; arr. © 2010 J. Orlando & P. Ringo. All Rights Reserved

Queen of Hearth and Home II

by Kathy Mac

Unseasonable gale-force winds blast rain between
her shingles and chimney.

The frozen dirt holds puddles against her home,
threatening the seam where cement ends, walls
begin.

Ground water leaches through the gaps between
gravel stones, tests the weep of her foundation.

But her house is old, strong.
Her friends, too.

In the night, each rises from bed to check the sump,
a reverse farce of non-encounters they laugh over in
      the morning.

After coffee, one pick-axes a drainage trench.
Another holds a ladder for the third who spreads
      tar along the roof-line.

While she scrambles a dozen eggs, toasts an entire
loaf of rye, and assembles a salad

by peeling wizened apples, shelling walnuts
left from the holidays. Crack. Crack.

Salmon Dorie Recipe
An Offering for Hestia

by Sparrow

It is logical to think that Hestia would like delicious, home-cooked food the best as offerings. I use this dish as an offering to Hestia. The below recipe is easy to make, and it's delicious. You can also use it the next day in sandwiches; it tastes even better the next day!

My Mom got this recipe from our local newspaper years ago, so I don't know who the original author is.

Recipe
2 tbsp cooking oil
½ tsp garlic powder (or 2 fresh cloves, minced)
2 tsp lemon juice, fresh or bottled
2 tsp dijon mustard
1½ lbs (680 g) fresh salmon fillets

Instructions
1. Stir cooking oil, garlic powder, lemon juice, and mustard together in a bowl.
2. Lay fillets in baking pan just large enough to hold single layer. Brush with all of garlic-lemon mixture.
3. Marinate at room temperature for 30 minutes, or cover and refrigerate for one hour.

4. Bake in 450°F (230°C) oven for 10 minutes per inch (2.5 cm) of thickness until fish flakes when tested with fork (which is 30 – 40 minutes).

Serves four.

Hestia's Domestic Bliss

by Verónica Pamoukaghlián

The virgin Hestia
the goddess of the hearth
builder of homes
saviour of mortgages

immune to lust
and all disputes
among the gods

the one who keeps
Olympus' peace

To live with Hestia
for eternity
— that was your plea —
in the surface perfection
of a home
with scenes of lust
and landscapes
painted on the walls

to create an illusion

to build the love
in a convenient place
and manufacture

perfect content
with the eroding lies
of every day

For Hestia's numbing peace
I will not sacrifice
my dream of bliss

My dream
even my dream alone
means more to me
than her reality

securities
and certainties
of those who share
Hestia's flameless bed

For fire is life
and certainty is death

An Unusual Holiday for Hestia in Roman Egypt
by P. Sufenas Virius Lupus

The syncretism of the Greek Goddess Hestia with the Roman Goddess Vesta is so well-known as to almost elude notice in most classical accounts and modern polytheists' perceptions. However, the syncretism of Hestia or Vesta with other Deities in other ancient Mediterranean cultures is far less frequent.

One such syncretism is that of Hestia with the Egyptian Nile Goddess Anoukis, which is witnessed in an inscription to various dual/syncretistic Deities from the second century BCE in Egypt on the island of Sehel.[1] The Deities included are Chnoubis-Ammon, Satis-Hera, Anoukis-Hestia, Petempamentes-Dionysos, Petensetis-Kronos, and Petensenis-Hermes. On the Neos Alexandria list, Edward Butler suggested the following based on the inscription:

The identification of Satis with Hera, and Anukis with Hestia, seems like a very interesting and intricate bit of theology. Most of the associations of Satis and Anukis have to do in one way or another with the Nile's annual inundation. I wonder whether the identification has something to do with Hestia being the first born of Kronos and the last disgorged. Could it be that the cycle of the inundation was somehow identified with Kronos devouring and disgorging his children? We have a local form of Kronos being worshiped at Sehel.[2]

I was thinking that the land is what is being "disgorged" by Kronos/the Nile when the waters recede. I note that Anukis is sometimes associated with the withdrawal of the waters, and consequently the sprouting of the seeds.[3]

This theological formation of the matter, therefore, relies not upon the usual identification of Hestia with fire and the communal hearth, and the life-giving nature of the waters of the Nile — apparently opposed though those elemental connections may seem — but instead upon the mythology and theogony of the children of Kronos. The typological connections between attributes of Deities in inter-pantheonic syncretism is not always as important as the similarities that emerge from the actual narratives in mythology of Deities.

However, Hestia has an entirely other manifestation in Egypt outside of Graeco-Egyptian syncretism. This manifestation is in a fragmentary cult calendar associated with the community of Tebtynis that comes from the mid-second century CE.[4] The calendar records a *dies natalis* ("birthday") festival for "Vesta" on December 11th, according to the editors/translators of the text;[5] the actual phrase is Greek, and reads *genéthlios Hestías*, "Hestia's birthday." But, what makes this festival even more noteworthy is that the festival is not even said to have been one held in Tebtynis, but instead in the community of Naukratis, the Egyptian emporium city founded by the pharaoh Amasis in the sixth century BCE on the Canopic branch of the Nile to facilitate trade and interaction with the Greek world, as noted by Herodotus.[6] And, what is stranger still is that Vesta/Hestia is not known to be one of the major Goddesses of Naukratis: Zeus, Hera, Apollon, Aphrodite, and the Dioskouroi are usually the major Deities associated with that particular city.

      Birthday celebrations for Deities are not uncommon in the Greek or Roman worlds. Examining Roman practice — since this calendar comes from the Roman period — we see that this festival is unprecedented in date from what had been established elsewhere. Roman practice does not record a *dies natalis* for Vesta, but it does mention a number of festivals to Her, including the Vestalia on June 9th (and other related occasions in June),[7] the rekindling of the fire of the Vesta's hearth in Rome by the Vestal Virgins on March 1st yearly,[8] and the participation of the Vestal Virgins in a number of other rituals during the year, often involving the making of the *mola salsa* for use in the rituals concerned (including Lupercalia on February 15th, Fordicidia on April 15th, Epulum Iovis on September 13th and November 13th, etc.).[9] But a festival for Vesta, much less a *dies natalis*, does not appear in the currently-available records at any point in December. Even if the Vestalia can be suggested as a festival particularly honoring (and named for) Vesta, there is nothing recording why Her festival is on that date. Ovid's *Fasti* has a lengthy entry for this day, detailing how Vesta escaped the advances of Priapus at a feast of the Gods hosted by Cybele through being warned by the braying of a mule, as well as many other interesting stories and customs associated with the Vestalia,[10] but there is no note on the significance of the day or its specific origins in his narrative.

Athenaeus of Naukratis, who wrote the *Deipnosophistae* in the later second century, does have a note on the *genéthlios Hestías* in Book IV. 149D-150B.

"In Naucratis," as Hermias says in the second book On the Gryneian Apollo, "the people dine in the town hall (prytaneion) on the natal day of Hestia Prytanitis and at the festival of Dionysus, and again at the great gathering in honour of the Comaean Apollo, all appearing in white robes which even to this day they call their 'prytanic' clothes. After reclining they rise again, and kneeling, join in pouring a libation, while the herald, acting as priest, recites the traditional prayers. After this they recline, and all receive a pint of wine excepting the priests of Pythian Apollo and of Dionysus; for to each of these latter the wine

is given in double quantity, as well as the portions of everything else. Thereupon each diner is served with a loaf of pure wheat bread moulded flat, upon which lies another loaf which they call oven-bread; also a piece of swine's flesh, a small bowl of barley gruel or of some vegetable in its season, two eggs, a bit of fresh cheese, some dried figs, a flat-cake, and a wreath. Any manager of the festival who provides more than these viands is fined by the censors, and what is more, neither are those who dine in the town hall permitted to bring in anything to eat, but they eat these foods alone, giving a share of what remains to the slaves. But on all other days of the year any diner who wishes may go up to the town-hall and eat, after preparing at home for his own use a green or leguminous vegetable, some salt-fish or fresh fish and a very small piece of pork; sharing these ... (he receives) a half-pint of wine. No woman may enter the town-hall except the flute-girl. Nor is it allowed to bring a chamber-pot into the town-hall either. If a Naucratite gives a wedding-banquet, it is forbidden, following the prescription of the marriage law, to serve eggs and honey-cakes."[11]

Hestia was very important in most Greek cities that had *prytanea*, and many older Greek cities in Egypt probably still had *prytanea* during the second century CE.[12] Further, Hestia/Vesta was very connected with the imperial family and its cultus from the time of Augustus/Octavian onwards would have given this festival in Egypt that much more of an important character during the imperial period.[13]

The cult calendar from Tebtynis from which this date comes features a number of festivals having to do with the imperial cultus, and in particular with dates of significance for the Emperor Hadrian, including his *vicennalia* (twenty years in the principate anniversary) in 136 marked on December 15th, and his *epibatéria* or "festival of first arrival" in Oxyrhynchus on November 29th and in Tebtynis on December 1st.[14] This calendar likely dates from the principate of Marcus Aurelius, c. 169-180 CE, since it honors Lucius Verus, with whom Marcus Aurelius was co-emperor from 161 until 169, as a *divus*.[15]

Given the Hadrianic interest of the overall calendar, it is also noteworthy that in the city of Antinoöpolis, which was founded by Hadrian in October of 130 CE in honor of his drowned-and-deified lover Antinous, Hestia is given honors in the deme named for Her under the phyla named after the emperor Nerva.[16] Because of Hadrian's well-known philhellenism, and the tendency of his successors to continue in many of these traditions, perhaps it was considered expedient to give greater attention to these festivals in honor of Greek divinities within the Graeco-Roman cities of Egypt during this period. Indeed, Athenaeus' description of the festivities observed for Hestia in Naukratis (as outlined by an earlier author) were probably written around the same time that this cult calendar was written, during the reign of Marcus Aurelius. Indeed, perhaps we owe the visibility of both the festival for Hestia's birthdate, and the description of its celebration quoted in Athenaeus, to the general atmosphere around this period in Graeco-Roman Egypt, when there was great concern to heighten Greek-derived religious activities in order to retain favor with the emperors.

No matter what the reason for the original preservation of these pieces of information happens to be, the two sources together — the Tebtynis imperial cult calendar, giving the specific dates; and the quotation in Athenaeus' *Deipnosophistae*, detailing the actual celebrations involved — is invaluable in giving a portrait of what Graeco-Roman citizens in Egypt did for a particular Goddess on an occasion deemed sacred to Her. Though it was a festival in which only, apparently, males took part (which in itself is an interesting contrast to the regular association of Vesta with women-only rituals and sacred sororities!), that does not have to be the case in the modern world, especially when the festival in question seems to be one of communal gathering and fellowship in honor of the Goddess rather than anything explicitly gender-based, gender-specific, or needlessly gender-exclusive. For those who practice Greek, Roman, Egyptian, or Graeco-Roman-Egyptian syncretistic paths, this information can be used easily in creating one's own observances of this festival, whether it celebrates Hestia, Vesta, or — in absence of any other dates known for Her — Anoukis.

Notes
1. Thomas Allan Brady, *Sarapis & Isis: Collected Essays* (Chicago: Ares Publishers Inc., 1978), pp. 30, 33.
2. http://groups.yahoo.com/group/neos_alexandria/message/31353
3. http://groups.yahoo.com/group/neos_alexandria/message/31368
4. S. Eitrem and Leiv Amundsen (eds.), *Papyri Osloenses III* (Oslo: Jacob Dybwad, 1936), §77, pp. 45-55.
5. Eitrem and Amundsen, pp. 50-51.
6. Robin Waterfield (trans.), *Herodotus: The Histories* (New York and Oxford: Oxford University Press, 1998), pp. 166-167 (2.178-179).
7. Lesley Adkins and Roy A. Adkins, *Dictionary of Roman Religion* (New York: Facts on File, 1996), p. 237.
8. Adkins and Adkins, pp. 237-238.
9. Adkins and Adkins, p. 238.
10. Sir James George Frazer (ed./trans.), *Ovid's Fasti* (Cambridge: Harvard University Press, 1931), pp. 338-355.

11. Charles Burton Gulick (ed./trans.), *Athenaeus, Deipnosophistae*, Volume 2 (Cambridge: Harvard University Press, 1928), pp. 182-185.

12. Eitrem and Amundsen, p. 50.

13. Eitrem and Amundsen, pp. 50-51.

14. P. J. Sijpesteijn, "A New Document Concerning Hadrian's Visit to Egypt," *Historia* 18 (1969), pp. 109-118 at 114; Eitrem and Amundsen, pp. 48-49; J. W. B. Barns, Peter Parsons, John Rea, and Eric G. Turner (eds.), *The Oxyrhynchus Papyri* Volume 31 (London: Egypt Exploration Society, 1966), §2553, pp. 72-77 at 76 lines 11-13; P. Sufenas Virius Lupus, *Devotio Antinoo: The Doctor's Notes, Volume One* (Anacortes: The Red Lotus Library, 2011), pp. 154-155.

15. Eitrem and Amundsen, p. 53.

16. Mary Taliaferro Boatwright, *Hadrian and the Cities of the Roman Empire* (Princeton: Princeton University Press, 2003), p. 194 note 124.

Hestia's Colors

by Rachel Iriswings

Organic brown and inky black
the darknesses beneath the house
Cement-white is the furnace, the pilot light glowing
       unknown

Trained-black the stovetop, rugged white the oven,
its workspace propane-black and cooked silver,
synthetic-yellowed as I reach inside

Dawn-yellow the kitchen walls
Fruit-splashed curtains, rugs, towels
Quiet gold handles on warm wood cabinets
just redder than my dog's fur

Loam-brown the couch and reclining chairs,
indifferent to pet hair blights
Cocoa-deep the rest they provide

Celestial-striped the sheets on my bed,
midnight the reversible blankets, zodiac-gilt the
       patterns
Snowing-sky-blue the walls and pillowcase,
just greener than my eyes

Blues intense to electric as the sun wakes with us,
a pastel catalyst feeding the dawn-walls

Amber-fire to ash as the day departs
through the grizzled blue horizon

Dusted silver that lifts Her breath from the
        basement
into my tired core as I lay on the bed
watching shy candles blush on my altar,
flickers smoothing the birch-white bookshelves
        above

Especially favored She is in these Michigan winters
Sun long gone, candle eyes closed, I lay on the bed,
my gaze to the indigo softened by ice-mirrored stars
The dusted breath always disputes the cold, but
only when the home sleeps can I hear Her hum

I sing "True Colors" in my head in response,
wondering if bright Iris helps Her decorate
or just helps me name Her honors …

To Hestia

by Karen Salvati Harper

Hestia
Silent flame of my heart
Quiet guardian of my inner sanctum
You are first and last
and all-pervading

Hestia
Steady fire of my hearth
Stately goddess with torch unwavering
Unencumbered
and all-embracing

Hestia
Burning bright in the dark
Subtle lady of veiléd wisdom
You are everywhere
and all-prevailing

Hymn to Hestia

Hestia, First and Last

by Amanda Artemisia Forrester

Hestia, first and last
Gentlest of the Olympians
The quiet one
She who tends the hearth
Goddess of home, of family, of hospitality
Peaceful harmony is her creed
So precious are the bonds of family to her
That when Apollo and Poseidon began to quarrel for
      her hand
She forsook marriage altogether
So as not to be the cause of conflict
Where before there had been only goodwill.
She desires not power or fame,
Neither does she feel the need to found her own
      dynasty
When there are already so many needy souls to
      attend to.
She is the heart of all things,
The axis round which we revolve,
The peaceful calm that all Gods cycle back to
(Eventually, when their tempestuous rages have
      ended)
And she calmly invites them back in,
For a hot meal and some pleasant conversation.
Hestia is the home,
She is the fire of love in our hearts,

The serenity of knowing where we stand
That we will always have a place to go to
As long as we can put aside our anger and make
          peace.
Hestia, so often overlooked,
Because she is deemed not "exciting" enough
Is very often the very thing we need most,
The fire most lacking in modern homes
Where the crackling fire has been replaced
By the glow of multiple smartphone screens
Where meals are eaten in silence
And the family no longer engages with each other
Please, gentle Goddess, return now to earth,
And teach us again the value of family and hearth
For we surely have need of you now.

Hymn to Hestia

by Leni Hester

First and last, we call to you, bright Hestia,
you who are the warm hearth and the water pitcher,
the empty chair and the resting spindle,
eldest and youngest child of time and space,
we ask your protection and blessing.
Secure our homes and protect our children,
be the warm welcome home at day's end
and the sweet haven of repose, gentle goddess,
guard our memories and fortify our walls,
trusty, radiant, kind, humble, and strong,
Hestia of the eternal flame, accept our prayers and
        offerings,
as we honor you, first and last.

In Praise of Hestia

by Lyssa Little Bear

Hail Hestia, goddess of hearth and home,
You who tend the sacred flame of Mount Olympus.
With oiled locks, you urge the fire to grow,
shedding light and warmth throughout the home of
      the gods.
Hestia, fire-keeper and fire-tender,
You are the guardian of the home,
who protects and shelters us from harm.
Chaste one, you guard your virginity fiercely,
preserving your own power and strength,
maintaining your own voice, beholden to no one
      save great Zeus.
You are first and last of the great gods,
born first to Kronos and Rhea, devoured first,
You emerged into this world last, the final god
saved by your brother
when he overthrew his father.
I give you praise, Hestia,
for you selflessly and ceaselessly tend the flame,
You guard our hearth, that we may honor the gods
before the sacred fire.
Hail Hestia, thank you for your blessings.

Hearthsong

by Jason Ross Inczauskis

We sing the praises of Hestia,
Noble goddess, and keeper of our home!
We are blessed, to have you with us,
For you keep our home fires burning while we
        roam!

May you call us safely back to you,
For you keep us warm in your embrace!
We give thanks for the sacred things you do,
And the blessings that you grant this mortal race!

We sing of beautiful Hestia!
Humble offerings to you we freely give!
May you watch over our loved ones,
And grant happiness in every day we live!

May you call us safely back to you,
For you keep us warm in your embrace!
We give thanks for the sacred things you do,
And the blessings that you grant this mortal race!

We sing of glorious Hestia!
The flame eternal, with fragrant oils you tend!
You're the heart of Mount Olympos,
And you hold the Earth so softly in your hands!

May you call us safely back to you,
For you keep us warm in your embrace!
We give thanks for the sacred things you do,
And the blessings that you grant this mortal race!

Darkness Bright

by Jay Logan

On that dark cold winter's night
Snow is slippery, now ice
Luminous light, all around
Has been banished, powered down

The only fire felt was in
Hearth and home and gentle grin
Huddled we round Hestia's flame
Ever bright did darkness reign

The ever-present glare, now gone
Air so silent, still, and soft
Stars above shone splendidly
Gods and heroes, plain to see

Prominent among them shone
The sinuous serpent, Draco
Darling dragon up on high
Round the polestar does she fly

Until now I had forgot
Great and gorgeous Tiamat
Mighty mother, torn and shred
Made the earth and firmament

Saw her there, I did then see
In the starlight, snow, and trees
Raiment of Rhea's milk led
Neck to body, tail to head

Ouroboros, wrapped around
All the cosmos, tail to crown
There for all who care to spy
On that dark cold winter's night

Goddess of Little Renown, But Lasting Prominence

by Elani Temperance

Modest goddess Hestia is the goddess of the hearth, family, fertility and the home. She's the goddess closest to the people, and was a very beloved goddess in ancient Hellas, even though she has little to no mythology to her name. Very few temples were dedicated (solely) to her, but the ancient Hellenes more than made up for this by making every home and every altar her abode. In order to understand Hestia's worship in ancient Hellas, we must paint a picture of ancient Hellenic life and note how engrained her worship and person were. A history lesson, then, on one of Hellas' kindest goddesses.

A Foreign Goddess Comes Home

The name Hestia, like that of her Roman counterpart Vesta, had become synonymous with anything related to family and houses. Many vacation homes carry the name, for example, promising a place of refuge and comfort in a foreign land. This is a legacy of hers that was established well over three thousand years ago in Persia, from where she seems to originate.

The Persians worshipped fire under the name 'ἑστια', which in turn was adopted by the ancient Hellenes and deified in the form of Hestia, meaning — strictly speaking — 'fire,' but which is usually translated as 'hearth,' 'hearth fire,' or 'fire side.' Many scholars now accept that Hestia was found in the fire of the hearth and not the other way around; the hearth in which the fire resides. She laughs as the fire crackles and all sacrifices are consumed by her flames. When oil and wine are poured over the altar, she leaps in acceptance of the sacrifice.

Goddess of Women, or Goddess of Men?

Caring for the household was a task solely intended for women. Most likely it is because of this that very few stories about Hestia were made or recorded; the male-dominated culture cared little for her.

Yet, it was the *kurios* who was charged with the tending of the home fire and retrieving it should it go out. Men who took the ephebic oath in Athens swore, among others, to Hestia to be good soldiers with all the attributes that came with it as they entered military service. Hence, every male Athenian citizen would have sworn it. It reaffirms the belief that Hestia was the symbolic heart of the city and thus worth fighting for and honoring, and shakes the traditional thought that Hestia was considered a female-oriented goddess.

Hestia's Place in the Home

Ancient Hellenic homes were simple structures made from clay, wood, and stone. The roofs were covered with tiles or reeds and the houses had one or two stories. Most houses were small, just a few rooms, with a walled garden or yard in the middle. Others were much larger. They were not solely homes, but often doubled as offices, shops, entertainment areas, and as a place of worship. In many cases a large wall with a single door connected the house to the street, which insured maximum privacy to the occupants of the house. Rooms at the front of the house often served as store rooms or workshops. Other rooms in the house served as bedrooms, kitchen, bathroom, and smaller storerooms. Symposia were held in special rooms, reserved only for men. The only women who entered the male-only rooms were serfs. These rooms were called *andron* (ανδρών).

Female-only rooms were called *gynaikon* (γυναικῶν). The women of the household — grandmothers, wives, and children, assisted by female serfs — would spend most of their time there, weaving, spinning, entertaining female friends and relatives and taking care of the children. Men were not allowed to enter these rooms and a visiting male guest would be punished most severely if he entered the *gynaikon*. Female serfs slept near the *gynaikon* in small, lightly-furnished rooms. Male serfs slept in similar rooms near the *andron*.

The courtyard of the home often held a *bômos*, a freestanding raised altar where the majority of household worship took place. Some houses also had a wall niche, an indoor worship area, either in a room especially designated for worship, or in the main family room. These altars were used to worship the *Ephestioi* (Εφεστιοι), the most personal of the household gods. These almost always included: Hestia, Zeus Ephestios (overseer of the hearth), Zeus Kthesios, and Agathós Daímōn. Worship at these altars was highly personal and many other gods could be added to this worship list, depending on the family and their needs.

Hestia was represented by the hearth fire that was always kept burning. All fires in the house were lit from this one fire so Hestia would watch over everything and everyone inside the house. She shared this task with Zeus Ephestios who was and is a more active defender of the home. He shields the actual structure of the house. Where Hestia watches over the occupants, Zeus Ephestios guards the very walls, the roof, the floor, and any possessions inside the structure. He was worshipped at the main altar.

When Every Home and City Becomes a Temple

Back in ancient Hellas, most religious activities surrounding the household revolved around the central hearth, which was watched over by Hestia as she is attributed with establishing the practice of building a home to live in with family. The male head of household, the *kurios*, presented serfs, children, and his new wife to the hearth fire so they became part of the *oikos* and fell under the protection of Hestia and the other household gods.

Oikos (οἶκος) is a fascinating Hellenic word meaning (or is the basis of) a multitude of things. Amongst others, *oikos* is linked to: a house (the material building), a household, family, lineage/descendants, palace, temple, and nation. This shows, once more, how interwoven family life, lineage, country, and religion were in ancient Hellas. *Oikos* has a clear relation to possession, yet there is also a religious component to it. It's linked to temples and, because it's also linked to the physical structure of the house, to the hearth and to Hestia.

Hestia's flame connected every single Hellenic *oikos* to each other and the state. All the household fires, temple flames, and those in government buildings were lit with a flame from the *prytaneion* (Πρυτανεῖον), the structure where state officials met and where the city kept a fire for Hestia burning day and night. Every single hearth fire in the city or town was linked to that central one, and that central fire was linked to the city from where the settlers of the new village, town, or city came. This network of fires, which was never allowed to go out, brought all Hellenes together.

This sense of connectivity was so engrained that if the hearth fire of a home went out, the male head of household would go to the *prytaneion* for a new flame.

Hestia as Goddess of Xenia

Hestia keeps the home fires burning and allows any *kurios* to act as a charitable host by offering any guest a place near the fire. Hospitality in ancient Hellenic society was a complicated ritual within which both the host and the guest had certain roles to fill and tasks to perform. Especially when someone unknown to the host came to the door, the ritual held great value. This, because any unknown traveler at the door could be a god or goddess in disguise, or they could even be watched over by a deity who would pass judgement on the host. This ritual practice of hospitality was called *xenia* (ξενία) and is described a lot in Hellenic mythology and ancient literary sources.

Very few people travelled in ancient Hellas outside of merchants and soldiers. When one chose to travel, they had a very good reason and as such it was assumed that shelter could always be found with good folk when needed. Hestia, from her position as the hearth, gave a weary traveler warmth, allowed the family to cook them food, boiled the water needed for the traveler to wash and to have his feet washed — a show of respect and honor — and at its very core, her light was a beacon to guide travelers who had been caught out after dark. The hearth's fire allowed the family to fulfill their part of the ritual practice of *xenia* and in return they were rewarded by the guest and, perhaps, by the gods as well.

Hestia's Mythological Lessons

While Hestia has little mythology to her name, what little mythology there is of her conveys all that the ancient Hellenes would have needed to know about her to give her worship, understand her place in the pantheon, and learn her lessons. Hestia's mythology focuses on two things: the fact that she was born 'both first and last' and that she was a virgin goddess, unwed and untainted.

In myth, Hestia was born first from Rhea and Kronos and thus first consumed when Kronos heard one of his children would usurp him. When Rhea gave him a drink to force him to regurgitate his children, Hestia appeared last as all children came forth in the sequence in which they had been swallowed. Because of this, she received both the first and last portion of sacrifice, a practice established in at least parts of ancient Hellas, and at the hearth, she received fatty portions of meat, bits of food, and droplets of wine at every meal.

Most of the gods are married and as such, Hestia was courted, as well. Both Apollon and Poseidon vied for her hand in marriage, but Hestia rejected them and fled to Zeus to beg him to remain a maiden all her days. Zeus accepted and installed her in the homes and temples of mankind instead where she would get the greatest honor from all: continuous worship and the best parts of a meal. One might assume this is simply an origin tale; a tale of why Hestia resides in the home. That is surely part of it, but there is a secondary — and far more important — lesson to be learned from this myth.

Ancient Athenian women were expected to marry, and they married young. Their husbands were often older, required to go through military training first and truly become a man. This meant that women were transient while men were not; fathers gave daughters away to another *oikos* and that daughter became a wife in the *oikos* of another. Sometimes they would establish an *oikos* of their own, but more often than not, women moved in with the entire family of the husband.

In ancient Hellas, or at least in ancient Athens, the unwedded daughters of the family tended to the hearth fire whenever it wasn't being used for religious purposes. Then it became the responsibility of the *kurios*, but it is still entirely possible that during the rites, the unmarried daughters of the *oikos* kept the fire burning. When no unmarried daughters were in the home, the youngest female took up the task. This meant that in the case of marriage, the person who tended Hestia's fire — and thus ensured her protection over the household — moved away or the task was shifted into the hands of another. For the ancient Hellenes this was a frightening concept because of the practice of *kharis*.

Kharis (χάρις) is one of the most important practices within Hellenismos and ancient Hellenic orthopraxy. *Kharis* is — to give an incredibly limited definition — the act of giving to the gods so they might give something in return. The ancient Hellenes gave sacrifice freely, joyfully, with pleasure, and out of respect and love for the gods. They asked what they felt they needed in prayer and never expected to be granted this request. Petitions weren't considered bribery; they gave to the gods and should they in turn feel inclined to grant those requests, the ancient Hellenes thanked them by offering to them again, to which the gods might respond, to whom they would sacrifice, and so on. This circular practice of voluntary giving is *kharis* and while it was established for the entire household during sacrifice, it was the unwedded daughter who got up early to tend to the fire, who pleaded to it as it sputtered, who sheltered it from the wind and sloshing of liquids and who dutifully added wood to it during all hours of the day.

There was always a little bit of fear that the family would lose a portion of the established *kharis* when the now-wedded daughter moved out and within the receiving family there was always uncertainty about how well the new addition could tend the fire and how much *kharis* she brought with her. Perhaps, they feared, it would upset the *kharis* the welcoming family had established. And so there came to be a mythological outlet for this fear, a placating story that took all doubts away: Hestia is a maiden goddess who was able to perform her duties and functions without being married and leaving her home. When the tender of the flame moved, Hestia remained behind. When a new addition was added to the family, she was introduced to the hearth as a clean slate and fell into the established traditions within the home, and its established *kharis*. Because Hestia is an unmarried goddess who is still able to oversee fertility and household stability, the transient nature of women in ancient Hellas was neutralized.

Hestia of the Oily Locks

Hestia's influence in daily life was felt — or rather smelled — in another way as well. In *Homeric Hymn 24 (To Hestia)* has the following line: 'with soft oil dripping ever from your locks'. It's an odd statement to make about a goddess from a modern perspective but in ancient Hellas, it was a great compliment.

To us the ancient world would most likely have been overpowering in terms of smell. The scent of sweat and animals filled a city's streets. Fragrance was everywhere in the ancient world, from scented oils used to adorn the body to incense burnt in homes and temples. To those who could afford it and in those areas where it was absolutely vital, like a temple, masking their odor and exuding a sweet scent was essential. For temples, incense was offered both during sacrifice and in intervals to keep the sweet smell vibrant, and this was done in Hestia's fire.

For personal use, perfumes were the way to go to ward off the stink. In the ancient world oils were used as the carrier medium for perfumes, where the medium today is alcohol. This must have meant that ancient perfumes were far less noticeable than modern ones and would have lain more thickly on the skin. The gods, obviously, must smell very, very sweet and thus Hestia would have pleasant-smelling oil literally 'dripping from her locks.' It can also refer to another thing: typical temple fires were lit not as a traditional hearth fire but in a lamp — an oil lamp. As such, the dripping oil from Hestia's locks could be a metaphor for the leaping flames from the fire of an oil lamp as well.

Hestia and Her Throne

There is a story floating about the internet and even some modern texts on Hellenic mythology, that Hestia gave up her throne to Dionysos. Apparently, this is an ancient myth, and the ancient Hellenes would have believed this as well. It's a story so frequently told, one that is such common knowledge, that very few people know the source. Well, the source is Robert Graves' *The Greek Myths*, written in 1955. From that book (27.12):

Finally, having established his worship throughout the world, Dionysus ascended into Heaven, and now sits at the right hand of Zeus as one of the Twelve Great Gods. The self-effacing goddess Hestia resigned her seat at the high table in his favor; glad of any excuse to escape the jealous wranglings of her family, and knowing that she could always count on a quiet welcome in any Greek city which it might please her to visit.

Graves provides two sources for this story: Apollodoros' *Bibliotheka* 3.5.3, and Pausanias' *Hellados Periegesis* 2.31.2. As you can read for yourself, there is no mention whatsoever of Hestia giving up her throne. In fact, the sources only address the part of Graves' text that follows afterwards, about Dionysos bringing his mother Semele up to Olympos as well. Plato, in his *Phaedrus* (246) states about Hestia's inclusion:

Zeus, the mighty lord, holding the reins of a winged chariot, leads the way in heaven, ordering all and taking care of all; and there follows him the array of gods and demigods, marshaled in eleven bands; Hestia alone abides at home in the house of heaven;

of the rest they who are reckoned among the princely twelve march in their appointed order.

Did Graves lie? Well, yes and no. Graves is a storyteller; he spun stories based on facts he could find. If he could not find a fact, he made it up to fit the story. Because of this, his books are a great read, but they are not reliable as far as ancient mythology goes. As for The Twelve; there was never a set grouping of them in ancient Hellas; what mattered was that there was a council of twelve, the Dodekatheon, at all. Who resided on the golden thrones was subject to debate, and varied per location.

The most canonical version of the Dodekatheon is represented in a relief which currently resides at the Walters Art Museum. The relief dates back to the 1st century BC to the 1st century AD and depicts the twelve Olympians carrying their attributes in procession: from left to right, Hestia (scepter), Hermes (winged cap and staff), Aphrodite (veiled), Ares (helmet and spear), Demeter (scepter and wheat sheaf), Hēphaistos (staff), Hera (scepter), Poseidon (trident), Athena (owl and helmet), Zeus (thunderbolt and staff), Artemis (bow and quiver), and Apollon (cithara). No mention of Dionysos.

Obviously, gods who were held in high regard in a certain city-state would have held the thrones, according to the people who lived in that city-state. This means that it's quite likely there were people in ancient Hellas who firmly believed that Dionysos occupied one of the thrones of the Dodekatheon. Most likely, there were also people who believed Hestia did not occupy one of the thrones. It's entirely possible that some people — perhaps even the same people who believed Dionysos was part of the Dodekatheon, but not Hestia — believed that Hestia gave up her seat to Dionysos. The problem is that there are no ancient sources to support this, and there was most certainly not a widespread myth to this effect that held sway in ancient Hellas.

Hestia, Goddess of All

Hestia's flame burned eternal in ancient Hellas. It burned in the heart of every city, in every temple and in every home. It was her flame that warmed and fed inhabitant and traveler alike. It was she that soldiers swore to protect when they enlisted, and it was she who bound all members of the *oikos* together, be they related by blood, marriage, or contract. Very few tales were told about her, but those that were cemented her influence in everyday life. She received the best and most frequent offerings of all the gods — as per her divine right — and in exchange she granted fertility, stability, and safety. Her influence was felt everywhere, but rarely exuberantly celebrated; there was no need to, as she was already honored by every single person in every single city in every single city-state. Her worship was universal and through that universality, it connected all men and women in the great Hellenistic empire that reigned supreme for many hundreds of years. And in all those years, it had Hestia as its heart.

Hestia of the Flame

by Amanda Artemisia Forrester

Hestia dwells in the center
The kind-hearted virgin Goddess
Tends the flame of Olympos

Wherever families come together
She is there
Wherever communities unite
She is there
Wherever an individual gives himself to others,
She is there

Hestia of the flame
The eternal fire
Unites all
She is the "we," never "I"
She is the center
The axis
Around which Olympos revolves

Hestia is the center of Olympos
Hestia is the heart of the family
Hestia is the hearth, the home
She is the calm within
Hestia is the glue
That holds societies together

Hestia dwells in the center
And we gather around her warmth

Hestia
(A Sixth Century Byzantine Tapestry)

My Covering Story
by Lyssa Little Bear

I had always been fascinated with the custom of covering one's hair. From when I was little, I would admire Muslim women in the street and compliment them on their hijabs. The patterns and colors of the scarves caught and held my attention. I also was very vain about my hair, and I spent quite a bit of time brushing it, trying new hairstyles, and trying to make it look perfect. I felt that my hair was my best feature, something that I could be proud of, something worthy of me spending a bit of time on it.

As I explored Paganism, becoming a devotee of Artemis, Athena and Hestia, I began to have conversations with the goddesses to whom I devoted my life.

Then Hestia came to me and started requesting that I cover my hair. The lady of the hearth did not give me a reason why, just that she would like me to do this until I learned the lesson she wanted to teach me. I am the kind of person who likes to know the why behind things, so it took a bit of repeating this request every time I decided to meditate. (I'm also kind of stubborn, it's a flaw I recognize.) I finally got the message a week later, and came up with my own reason why the goddess wanted me to cover. I thought that the lesson was learning modesty, and went at this new adventure with good spirit.

I immediately hit flak from my blood family, who questioned my motives, and on one occasion mocked my tichel-style head covering, saying, "You look like you came from a chemo ward." That hurt, but what hurt more was the sense that by mocking my decision to cover, they were ridiculing my religious choice. The one person who was the most supportive in all of this was my then-fiance, now-husband, Rune. He was my rock through the time I was covering. Whenever I was discouraged by my blood family's reaction, I could turn to him and instantly feel better.

The fact that I hit flak so soon after starting to cover made me question my act of devotion. I chose to listen to the goddess of the hearth and do something that would further my spiritual path. It threw in my heavily Christian family's face my Paganism, something that they could ignore as I was living away from home. My covering brought my religious choice to the forefront of their mind when they saw me. I got a lot of comments from my mother of, "I miss your hair." That hurt, but I felt that Hestia would not lead me wrong. There was something to be gained from this experience. I just had to find out what it was.

I covered my hair for a year and three months, amassing a large collection of scarves and in turn becoming just as prideful and vain about how my cover looked as I was how my hair used to look. It was one day in December, right before the winter solstice, that I realized where my mindset had gone. I immediately sought the advice of my goddess. The fire keeper made it clear that I had learned the lesson she wanted me to learn.

I needed to eliminate my vanity and pride.

That lesson was not one I had expected. I thought that she wanted me to be more modest in my dress, and had focused on that for the year and three months that I covered. Coming to terms with the fact that I was a human, capable of vanity and pride, was a lesson that Hestia felt I needed to learn, and by the gods, did I learn it. By taking away the thing that I was most prideful over, my hair, it taught me that I had worth in other areas. I would overlook things I was good at or features I could appreciate in favor of my hair. I was not my hair, I had value in other areas.

As I had been wondering for a couple of months whether or not I needed to keep covering, the goddess Hestia informed me that since I learned the lesson she was trying to teach me, I was free to stop covering. As of now, I do not cover my hair.

I strive to keep the humble attitude Hestia taught me while I was covering. I learned a lot about myself during that time period. I never thought that I would recognize my vanity, but Hestia showed me there is more to life than being wrapped up in your personal appearance. It was a humbling experience but one that I feel I needed.

Thank you, lady of the hearth, goddess of the home, for showing me that I am more than my appearance. I am more than just one facet of myself.

I have value, I have worth, I matter.

Thank you, Hestia.

Prayer to Hestia

by Merit Brokaw

Lady Hestia, goddess of the hearth,
wrapped in a himation of fire
I honor thee and seek thy blessings
for my home, family, and community.
You are the first born of Rhea
and the last disgorged by Kronos.
Virgin eternal having denied all suitors,
even the lords Apollo and Poseidon.
By belonging to none, you belong to all.
Builder of dwellings, paired with Hermes,
I ask that you protect my home.
As the center of domestic life and
the giver of domestic blessings,
you are the heart of every home.
Be welcome in my home always.
At your altar, all offerings are laid.
There all the divine ones gather,
giving you the first portion.
Doubly welcome, are you,
for the company that you keep.
May your harmonious ways
influence my family, near and far.
As your fire is the center of the home,
so is your altar the center of community.
It is a place for coming together
where differences do not matter

where asylum can be found.
May you bless my community
with peace and unity.
As Gaia contains a molten core,
so all of humanity rings your flame.
May you turn all of humanity
into one large community
through tolerance and compromise
minimizing or reversing damage
to Gaia and to her children.
I honor thee lovely lady of light and warmth.
I pray that your blessings ignite
within one and all, now and forever.
Make it so through truth and love.
Hail Lady Hestia!

The Hearth as Witness

by Gerri Leen

The soft purr of the cat
On the hearth
The slow creak of
The rocking chair
Before the fire
Logs shifting as I consume
Scents of life burning
The resiny taste of cypress
The snap-crack of laurel
The whisper-life of grass

I hear the sigh of the human
Warmth spreading through old bones
I have watched her always
Learning to walk, to talk, to sing
To love, to fall, to birth, to cry
And finally, to die
But not today
Today I will keep her safe
If she cannot get up
To feed me
I will burn the air itself
Just this once
For her

The cat purrs

It is not a sound of joy
He knows his mistress falters
His purr is self-comfort
He inches closer to me
I feel his need
I cannot save her
So I burn brighter
And he stretches out
Emerald eyes closing
The soft kiss of love's glance
As he watches her breathe
In and out, in and out
Her breath as raspy as
A wildfire
As unfulfilling as a
Flame burning only paper

She stares into the fire
I stare back
We wait

Hestia, The Heart of the Cosmic Order

by Ann Hatzakis

In the "ordinary" view of Hestia's role in the order of the Olympian *theoi*, she is usually overlooked as she is not what people think of as an "important" goddess. She is not flashy. She is quiet, and it is that quietness that makes people unaware of her importance in the combined roles of the three daughters of Kronos.

While Hera is the goddess who is responsible for a lot of the inspiration for human governance and Demeter the one who is responsible for agricultural pursuits, Hestia is the one who governs the center of all human endeavors, the hearth and home.

Without the home, all other human endeavors become a lot more shaky as they have no firm foundation. Without Hestia and her "cosmic hearth," all other endeavors of the *theoi* have no firm base either.

In Hellenismos, the *oikos* (household) is where all of the most basic rituals of life occur. When a child is born, they are introduced to the *oikos* at a real or symbolic hearth. When a marriage happens, it is symbolically the creation of a new hearth at the heart of the new *oikos*. When a death happens, if we were to mirror the ancient practice, the fire in the hearth is temporarily extinguished as the *theoi* are not seen around miasma.

The rituals in the *oikos*, the rituals of daily life, are central to Hellenismos as they provide the foundation of our faith. The public rituals, while important, are not what provides the means to pass on the religion's basic practices to future generations. What public rituals do is link the various households together into a greater community. When there is not a way to actually do public rituals due to a lack of available households for it, there are still the household rituals to honor the theoi.

Hestia is honored both first and last in both the public and household rites. Why would this be the case if there were not a reason? Perhaps it is because Hestia is more important than many people give her credit for; after all, she is both the hearth and the fire in the hearth. Without that fire, offerings to the Olympian *theoi* are not made (with the exception of libations, which are still done in front of Hestia's flame). According to the Homeric hymn honoring Hestia, no feast happens where she is not honored. We should remember this as we go through our lives.

Some of the things that people have mentioned to me since the writing of a blog post on Hestia being at the center of the *oikos* is that the *oikos* itself is central to any sort of society; it is at the center of what it means to be civilized. Without the stable center that the household provides, you cannot have a neighborhood, much less a polis. Without the polis, you cannot grow states, much less nations.

It is telling that in ancient times — in the Hellenic world at least — when people left one city to found another they took fire from the central hearth of the city they were leaving to use in lighting the central hearth of the new city. This made the new city an extension in some ways of the older one.

The importance of the central hearth of the polis is that it was a way to provide a "pure" flame to restart the fire of an individual *oikos*, in the case of it having to be extinguished due to the miasma of a death within the walls of that *oikos*. It is in some ways the symbol of the central hearth of the *oikos* of the Olympian *theoi*, and as such expresses the agency of Hestia throughout the life of the polis and also within the framework of the Olympians.

Hestia is often underestimated by modern Hellenic Polytheists because there is a lack of information about her cultus in ancient times, other than the acknowledgment that she is to be honored at the beginning and end of any rite. However it is this very acknowledgment that is an indicator of how important she actually was in ancient times. One thing that many scholars tend not to write about is the everyday things that they encounter, because "common knowledge" is not something that most people think would be lost in the event of a major cultural shift.

However, if you look at modern Greek culture, you can still see a remnant of Hestia's importance in the importance that is given to hospitality. When a guest enters the home, they are offered food and drink, things that are in Hestia's domain as the hearth is where those things are/were prepared. Even with the cultural shift that occurred due to the forcible Christianization of Greek society, some elements of the older polytheistic traditions remain within the minds of the common people.

This is actually evident in the way that modern Greeks are banding together to help one another during the economic trials the country is going through right now. Hestia is inspiring community even now, whether most people realize it. It is also evident in the way that the common people of the Greek islands are helping refugees coming from war-torn areas. This is well within the boundaries of hospitality in the ancient Hellenic traditions. We should not do any less for people in our own areas who need the blessing of community as it is one of the truest ways to honor the goddess at the heart of the cosmic order.

Hymn to the Fire of Naukratis

by P. Sufenas Virius Lupus

The Gods of Naukratis praise the Goddess of Their hearth-fire,
Hestia, the sustainer of life and warmth, on the day of Her birth.

First to praise Her is Zeus, youngest brother of the Goddess,
Whose heavenly fire is fed from Her hearth-fire.

Second to praise Her is Hera, younger sister of the Goddess,
without Whose fire no marriage can be enacted.

Third to praise Her is Aphrodite, great-aunt and niece of the Goddess,
Whose love in hearts is sustained by fire in hearths.

Fourth to praise Her is Apollon, nephew of the Goddess,
Whose insight is made possible by Her hearth.

Fifth to praise Her are the Dioskouroi, nephews of the Goddess,
Who carry the fire of the Goddess in Their torches on horseback.

Sixth to praise the Goddess is Anoukis, Her sister,
Who pours forth from the Nile the good things of
   life.

Seventh to praise the Goddess is Satis, Her mother,
Who pursues the good things of life in the hunt.

Eighth to praise the Goddess is Hathor, Her sister,
Who with dance and beer makes the good things
   of life.

Ninth to praise the Goddess are the Two Sobeks,
   Her nephews,
Who guard Her fire and all the good things of life.

Tenth to praise the Goddess is Horus, Her nephew,
Who brings Her fire and the good things of life to
   other lands.

Eleventh to praise the Goddess is Amun, Her
   grandfather,
Who in His obscurity depends on Her fire for the
   good things of life.

Twelfth to praise Her, the Goddess Hestia in
   Naukratis,
is Antinous, Her grandson, the flood of the good
   things of life.

May all the Gods of the Two Lands, the Mainland
 and Isles and Colonies,
in Greece and in Egypt, praise Hestia at Her birth in
 Naukratis!

Haikus for Hestia

by Rebecca Buchanan

I
heart of the
home:
burning bright

II
a seat at the hearth:
stranger and
friend ever welcome

III
she is the warm and
welcoming heart
of every true home

Hestía: An Acrostic

by T.J. O'Hare

Her attributes are multitudinous, hidden,
Even subtle; and not publicly acknowledged
So that the secrets she brings are so easily
Taken for granted. The fire that burns breezily
In its sacred hearth gives goodness that has voyaged
Across titanic gulfs, to do her will as bidden.

O Keeper of the Flame
by Lyssa Little Bear

O goddess who tends the fire,
burning brightly in the hearth of the gods,
on high Mount Olympus,
I cry your praises.
O goddess of the flame,
You feed the fire,
that the sacred pyre may never extinguish,
caring for the embers until they burst into life.
O goddess bathed in flickering light,
the crackle of wood is your symphony,
the hiss and pop of tinder, your chorus,
the sputter of timber, your music.
O goddess Hestia,
Your warmth and radiance shine from every flame,
every candle, every fireplace, every bonfire,
anywhere a flickering torch is kindled,
you are there.

In Honour of Hestia
by Ariadni Rainbird

Hestia, blessed queen,
Mystic virgin most serene,
Selfless one, untouched and pure
Self-contained, mild, demure.
Duty-bound, you tend the flame
The sacred fire, from whence all came.
The demiurge, the creative power,
Exciting, enlivening, Zeus's great tower
The sacred flame within the soul,
That moves us, pushes us to be whole
As you are whole within yourself
The perfect circle, the heart and hearth.
First and last, we pray to you
Accept our offerings, ever true.
And your mystics, deign to bless
with wisdom, health, and happiness.

To Hestia

by Jessi Robinson

You are the brightly-burning eternal flame of the
    gods.
The warming hearth providing mortal life,
The inspiration that lights the soul.
Your offerings are first and last
To honor your status amongst your siblings.
I honor your name
And place you at the center of my home
That it may have your protection
And I may receive your blessing.

Prayer to Hestia, To Be Spoken By the Dying

by Alexeigynaix

Bright goddess of the hearth and home,
I pray to you a final time.
If ever I have offered you
the first and last libations, then
please keep my loved ones safe from harm.
May those who'd soothe their grief and pain
show them they're welcome at their homes.
I ask they find support they need
and understanding friends to help
as life goes on. I ask at last
that I may be remembered for
the joys I brought to those I knew,
and that my deeds live always on;
remember me, O Hestia.
I thank you and bid you farewell.

*[Note: In Robert Garland's **The Greek Way of Death** (pages 14 and 16), Garland says one of the features common to Greek preparation for death is a prayer to Hestia. He quotes Euripides's **Alkestis** making such a prayer. This is inspired by that quote.]*

The First and the Last

by Sparrow

You were the first born.
You were ripped from Your mother's loving arms,
And devoured by Your father as if You were a piece
ของ delicious meat.

In Your father's stomach You were alone,
Until Your two sisters and two brothers joined You.
How happy You must have been to finally have
family with You.
But then You were alone again when Your sisters
and brothers were thrown up.

Alone again …

What did You see and feel, gentle Goddess
When You were alone in Your father's cavernous
stomach?

I am no shaman or priest, so I cannot say.
I can only imagine that in the darkness You saw the
Holy Fire,
The Sacred Flame,
That belongs to You and is You.
That Holy Fire kept You safe
Not even powerful Kronos could extinguish it.
Nor could he fight Fate.

For then You were the last to be thrown up.
Your brother Zeus rescued You from Kronos
I imagine He kindly smiled at You and said:
"Rise, eldest sister! Rise and be the shining Goddess You are! Join Me and Our siblings! Let's go to Mount Olympus and be the new reining Gods. Our brothers and I will fight Kronos and the Titans. We will establish a new, just order."

You smiled warmly at Zeus and said:
"Oh, mighty brother! How I love You and Our family! I will sit and guard the hearth at Olympus while You battle the Titans. Remember, I will always be at the Hearth. Even if one day Olympus should fall, I will be there, for I am the First and the Last."

Hestia by Laurie Goodhart

Appendix A: Epithets of Hestia
compiled by Chelsea Luellon Bolton

English Epithets
Blessed
Blessed, Holy and Divine
Chief of the Goddesses
Daughter of Kronos
Daughter of Rhea
Divine
Goddess of the Hearth
Gold-Throned
Guardian of the Innermost Things
Eternal
Fair Goddess
First-Born Daughter
First-Born of Wily Kronos
Florid Queen
Holy
Lovely
Queenly Maid
Sister of All-Highest Zeus
Who Dwells Among Great Fire's Eternal Flame
You Who Increase the Great Prosperity
Modern Titles
Eternal-Virgin
Glorious Goddess
Goddess of the Hearth and Hearth-Fire
Goddess of the Home's Hearth

Goddess of the Public Hearth
Goddess of the Royal Hearth
Great Goddess
Lady of All Altars
Lady Given Honors by Zeus
Lady of the Hearth-Fire
Lady of the Home
Lady of All Sacrifices to the Gods
Sister of Hades
Sister of Hera
Sister of Poseidon
Sister of Zeus
Veiled Goddess
Who Hears All Prayers
Who Receives the First and Last Offerings

Sources
The Homeric Hymns: A Translation, with Introduction and Notes. Translated by Diane Rayor. University of California Press, 2004.
The Orphic Hymns: Text, Translation and Notes, trans. By Apostolos N. Athanassakis. Johns Hopkins University Press, 2013.
Theoi Project
http://www.theoi.com/Ouranios/Hestia.html

Appendix B: Public Domain Hymns to Hestia

Homeric Hymn 29 to Hestia (trans. Evelyn-White) (Greek epic C7th - 4th B.C.):
Hestia, in the high dwellings of all, both deathless gods and men who walk on earth, you ahve gained an everlasting abode and highest honour: glorious is your portion and your right. For without you mortals hold no banquet,--where one does not duly pour sweet wine in offering to Hestia both first and last. And you, Argeiphontes [Hermes], son of Zeus and Maia, . . . be favourable and help us, you and Hestia, the worshipful and dear. Come and dwell in this glorious house in friendship together; for you two, well knowing the noble actions of men, aid on their wisdom and their strength. Hail, Daughter of Kronos (Cronus), and you also, Hermes.

***

Homeric Hymn 24 to Hestia:
Hestia, you who tend the holy house of the lord Apollon, the Far-shooter at goodly Pytho, with soft oil dripping ever from your locks, come now into this house, come, having one mind with Zeus the all-wise — draw near, and withal bestow grace upon my song.

***

Orphic Hymn 84 to Hestia (trans. Taylor) (Greek hymns C3rd B.C. to 2nd A.D.):

To Hestia, Fumigation from Aromatics. Daughter of Kronos (Cronus), venerable dame, who dwellest amidst great fire's eternal flame; in sacred rites these ministers are thine, mystics much blessed, holy and divine. In thee the Gods have fixed their dwelling place, strong, stable basis of the mortal race. Eternal, much formed, ever florid queen, laughing and blessed, and of lovely mien; accept these rites, accord each just desire, and gentle health and needful good inspire.

Appendix C: Our Contributors

Alexeigynaix is not a priest yet, but they intend to be. Their list of art, craft, and writing projects is ever-growing and never-ending. They run the Delmarva Nikephoros Proto-Demos of Hellenion.

Chelsea Luellon Bolton has a BA and an MA in Religious Studies from the University of South Florida. She is the author of *Lady of Praise, Lady of Power: Ancient Hymns of the Goddess Aset*, *Queen of the Road: Poetry of the Goddess Aset*, and *Magician, Mother and Queen: A Research Paper on the Goddess Aset*. She is the editor and a contributor of the forthcoming anthology *She Who Speaks Through Silence: A Devotional Anthology for Nebet Het (Nephthys)*. Her poetry has been previously published in various anthologies. She lives with tons of books and her anti-social feline companion. You can read more of her work at her blog address: http://fiercelybrightone.com

Wife, Mother, Librarian, Devotee to Zeus, Isis and Heru-ur, Housewife, Writer, Crafter and Woman. **Merit Brokaw** is an octopus with many tentacles of interest making her way through the sea of life. Author Blog: OakenScrolls.wordpress.com.

Rebecca Buchanan is the editor of the Pagan literary ezine, *Eternal Haunted Summer*. She is also the editor-in-chief of *Bibliotheca Alexandrina*. She has been previously published, or has work forthcoming, in *Bards and Sages Quarterly*, *Eye to the Telescope*, *Faerie Magazine*, *The Future Fire*, and other venues. She has published two short story collections with *Asphodel Press*: *A Witch Among Wolves, and Other Pagan Tales*; and *A Serpent in the Throat, and Other Pagan Tales*.

A practicing polytheist for over twenty-five years, **Edward Butler** received his doctorate from the New School for Social Research in 2004 for his dissertation "The Metaphysics of Polytheism in Proclus." Since then, he has published numerous articles in academic journals and edited volumes, primarily on Platonism and Neoplatonism and on polytheistic philosophy of religion, as well as contributing essays to several devotional volumes. He also writes a regular column, Noēseis, for Polytheist.com, and is an associate editor of *Walking the Worlds: A Biannual Journal of Polytheism and Spiritwork*. More information about his work can be found at his site: https://henadology.wordpress.com/.

Nicholas D. Cross holds undergraduate and graduate degrees in religion and ancient history. His interest in Hestia stems from his doctoral work on the social and religious influences upon interstate relations in ancient Greece. His research interests include Greek and Roman history, interstate relations, ancient religions, numismatics, historiography, and Greek and Latin languages. He currently lives and teaches ancient history in New York City.

Amanda Artemisia Forrester is currently working on building the Missouri homestead of her dreams. She is the author of *Ink In My Veins: A Collection of Contemporary Pagan Poetry*, and *Songs of Praise: Hymns to the Gods of Greece*. She is working on the forthcoming *Journey to Olympos: A Modern Spiritual Odyssey*. A self-labeled history geek, she has taught classes on Greek Mythology, contacting your spirit guides, and has written and taught the coursework for "Olympos in Egypt", an introduction to the unique hybrid culture and spiritually that grew up in Alexandria, Egypt in the Hellenistic Age. In a few years when the homestead is up and running, she may make it her goal to begin teaching again and holding rituals on her five acre property, Artemis Acres, and reestablish the Temple of Athena the Savior (formerly of South Bend, Indiana) in Missouri. Her blog can be found at templeofathena.wordpress.com, and she runs a Cafepress store, OtherWorld Creations, at cafepress.com/other_world.

All her life, **Tina Georgitsis** has maintained a deep love and appreciation for the mystical, whilst also being deeply respectful to the Ancient Greek and Ancient Egyptian spiritual/magickal paths which she is devoted to. She is an Arch Priestess Hierophant within the Fellowship Of Isis (Lyceum of Heka), Hereditary Folk/Hermetic Witch, Initiated Wiccan Priestess and runs the Sanctuary of Hekate's Crossroads (a temple devoted to Hekate) and is the owner of Hekate's Crossroads (a popular Facebook group devoted to Hekate). Qualified as a Reiki, Seichim and Sekhem Master and Tarot Councillor with the ATA, Tina has also studied various modalities within natural/alternative medicine and has worked professionally as a reader, healer, purveyor of magickal items and teacher of workshops in various metaphysical and occult subjects. Tina Georgitsis has been published in several varied publications over the years, ranging from anthologies, magazines and blogs. A regular article writer focusing on Kemetic, Hellenic and general occult works, she also edited her first book, *Daughter of the Sun: A Devotional Anthology in Honor of Sekhmet,* in 2015.

Laurie Goodhart writes: For the past thirty years I have divided my professional life between artwork and sustainable agriculture. The two come together beneath the surface as I continue to sift through the remaining evidence of ancient worlds, trying to sense how people of lost cultures met basic survival needs and how they responded to the very human hunger for beauty, meaning, and story.

Karen Salvati Harper is a writer living in South Carolina. Her poem, "Queen of Swords," appeared in *Arcana: The Tarot Poetry Anthology* (*Minor Arcana Press*, 2015). She also blogs about mental health on TheMighty.com. Follow Karen's Tarot adventures at seachangetarot.com.

Ann Hatzakis is a mother, a part-time blogger and has been a devotee of the Hellenic Pantheon since the mid-1980s.

Allie Hayes is a Hellenic polytheist and hedgewitch living in New Hampshire.

Leni Hester is a Witch, writer, and priest living and serving the orishas and the ancestors in Denver, Colorado. A frequent contributor to magazines *SageWoman* and *Witches & Pagans*, her work also appears in *Bearing Torches* and *Queen of the Great Below* (*Bibliotheca Alexandrina*), *Women's Voices in Magick*, and volumes one and two of *The Pop Culture Grimoire* (*Immanion Press*).

Jason Ross Inczauskis completed his Masters degree in Plant Biology and is currently residing in Southern Illinois. He currently lives in a small house with his love, Tabitha, and more books and dolls than you can shake a stick at. He has worshipped Athena since the year 2000, and gradually came to worship the other Hellenic deities as well, officially converting to Hellenismos in 2010. When asked about his spiritual path, he may refer to himself as a Hellene, a Hellenic Polytheist, an Orphic, or Greek Pre-Orthodox, depending on who's asking and his mood at the time, though he always follows it with the caveat: 'but not a very good one'. He is the editor for *Shield of Wisdom: A Devotional Anthology in Honor of Athena*. His devotional writing has also appeared in *He Epistole*, as well as several books, including *From Cave to Sky: A Devotional Anthology in Honor of Zeus*, *Queen of Olympos: A Devotional Anthology for Hera and Iuno*, *Harnessing Fire: A Devotional Anthology in Honor of Hephaestus*, *Guardian of the Road: A Devotional Anthology in Honor of Hermes*, *Out of Arcadia: A Devotional Anthology in Honor of Pan*, *Unto Herself: A Devotional Anthology for Independent Goddesses*, *The Scribing Ibis: An Anthology of Pagan Fiction in Honor of Thoth,* and *The Shining Cities: An Anthology of Pagan Science Fiction*.

Rachel Iriswings has been a Solitary Eclectic Neopagan since Samhain 2011, but has narrowed her focus to the ancient Greek pantheon and is currently building relationships with the Theoi as a non-reconstructionist Hellenic Polytheist.

David W. Landrum lives and writes in West Michigan, USA. His stories and mythological writings have appeared widely.

Jennifer Lawrence has followed the gods of Greece, Ireland, and the Northlands for decades now; she is a member of Hellenion, The Troth, Ár nDraíocht Féin, and Ord Brigideach. After earning a B.A. in Literature and a B.S. in Criminal Justice, she went on to work as an editor for Jupiter Gardens Press, a small publishing company in the Midwest. Her interests include history, gardening, herbalism, mythology and fairy tales, hiking, camping, and the martial arts. Her work has appeared in numerous publications, including *Aphelion, Jabberwocky, Cabinet Des Fees, Goblin Fruit, Idunna, Oak Leaves*, and many devotional anthologies. She lives with five cats, an overgrown garden full of nature spirits, and a houseful of gargoyles somewhere outside of Chicago.

Gerri Leen lives in Northern Virginia and originally hails from Seattle. She has work appearing in: *Nature, Flame Tree Press*'s *Murder Mayhem* and *Dystopia Utopia* anthologies, *Daily Science Fiction, Escape Pod, Grimdark*, and others. She recently caught the editing bug and has finalized her third anthology for an independent press. See more at http://www.gerrileen.com.

Lyssa Little Bear is the Demarkhos of the Apple Blossom Proto-Demos of Hellenion, a devotee of Artemis, Hestia, and Hermes, and an oath-bound Dedicant of Zeus. She lives in Michigan and is married to a Northern Tradition Celtic Polytheist. Together they are owned by two cats. Lyssa intends to begin clergy training through Hellenion soon and in her spare time she likes to craft and write.

Jay Logan is a long-time resident of the Pacific Northwest in the would-be sovereign state of Cascadia. He is an initiated priest of Chalice Hart, a local Wiccan coven, as well as a mystes of the Naos Antinoou, which he serves as a Mystagogue. A librarian by trade, he enjoys reading, providing information and resources to the public, knitting, and dancing in moonlight at the Witches' Sabbat.

P. Sufenas Virius Lupus is metagender, and is one of the founders (though no longer a member) of two major modern Antinoan groups, and practices a queer, Graeco-Roman-Egyptian syncretist reconstructionist polytheist devotion dedicated to Antinous, the deified lover of the Roman Emperor Hadrian and related divine figures. E is also a contributing member of the Neos Alexandria group, and a practicing Celtic Reconstructionist polytheist in the filidecht and gentlidecht traditions of Ireland (with further devotions to Romano-British, Gaulish, and Welsh Deities), and a devotee of several divine Ancestors and Land Spirits in the area of western Washington state. To date, Lupus' work has appeared in the *Bibliotheca Alexandrina* devotional anthologies for Artemis, Hekate, Isis and Serapis, Zeus, Pan, Thoth, Persephone, the Virgin Goddesses, the Near Eastern Deities, Hermes, Hephaistos, the Morrígan, the Muses and Graces, Charon, Hera/Juno, Demeter, Bast, Sekhmet, and the science fiction and sacred journey anthologies with further forthcoming work to appear in the devotional volumes for the Dioskouroi, Athena, Mars, and the Cynocephalic Deities, as well as others. Lupus' essays, fiction, and poetry have also appeared in many publications and periodicals; e is also the founder of *The Red Lotus Library*, and has published six books through it — most recently *The Antinoan Mysteries: The Founding, Fate, Failure, Fall, and Finish of a Modern Mystery Cult* (2016), with further volumes soon to be released. Lupus also published *The Phillupic Hymns* in 2008 with *Bibliotheca Alexandrina*. Lupus contributes a column to Polytheist.com called "Speaking of Syncretism." E is also on the editorial board of the polytheist journal *Walking the Worlds*.

Kathy Mac's poetry books are *Human Misunderstanding, The Hundefräulein Papers*, and

Nail Builders Plan for Strength and Growth, all of which are published with *Roseway Press*. Mac teaches creative writing at St. Thomas University in Fredericton, NB, Canada.

T.J. O'Hare writes short stories, novels, song lyrics, poetry, plays and film scripts. His novel *Amnesiak: Blood Divinity* published by *Spero Publications* is at https://www.smashwords.com/books/view/260414. He co-writes with many musical collaborators. His plays have been staged in Northern Ireland and Belgium. He is married to Jean, and has two grown-up sons. He lives in the north of Ireland.

Jessica Orlando opted not to provide a biography.

Verónica Pamoukaghlián is a freelance journalist, a novel translator for Amazon Publishing and an IBERMEDIA Scholarship recipient. Her literary work in various genres has appeared in *The Acentos Review, Prism, Naked Punch, The Galway Review, The Southern Pacific Review, Sentinel Literary Quarterly*, and elsewhere. She has been a guest lecturer at the University of Louisville, Kentucky, and a Creative Writing professor at Uruguay´s Technical University.

Devon Power opted not to provide a biography.

Ariadni Rainbird writes: I am a psychologist, witch, pagan priestess and for the last few years, follower of an Orphic tradition. The Hellenic Gods have always been with me, since childhood, when I read the myths and tales of heroes as my bedtime reading, and they captured my imagination and my heart. I went on to study and explore many different paths in adulthood, but the Hellenic Gods have always called to me the strongest, and I feel I have now come full circle in my path, returning to those childhood stories, but with a deeper understanding and more serious study and honour of the Gods.

Peter Ringo opted not to provide a biography.

At the age of twelve, **Jessi Robinson** convinced her parents to stop attending CCD as she didn't feel right getting confirmed as a Catholic when she didn't believe in the religion. Ten years later, she turned toward the Greek gods, whose mythos had been part of her life since childhood, with a particular devotion to Hermes, Athene, and Hephaistos. Today, she practices Greek Polytheism with a focus on Reconstruction in practice and Neo-Platonic-Buddhism in philosophy. Jessi lives with her wife and their menagerie of pets in a home surrounded by trees in southern Massachusetts.

Eric Paul Shaffer is author of six poetry books, including *A Million-Dollar Bill*, published in 2016 by *Grayson Books*. Other volumes are *Lāhaina Noon*; *Portable Planet*; and *Living at the Monastery*, *Working in the Kitchen*, and a novel *Burn & Learn*. 450 of his poems appear in reviews in Australia, Canada, England, Ireland, New Zealand, Wales, and the USA. Shaffer received the 2002 Elliot Cades Award for Literature and teaches at Honolulu Community College.

Sparrow is a solitary pagan with Buddhist leanings. She first fell in love with the Greek Gods and Goddesses when as a child she read *D'Aulaires' Book of Greek Myths*. Her love of Greek mythology introduced her to the second greatest love of her life: reading. Sparrow also likes going to plays and movies, and traveling.

Elani Temperance is practicing Hellenist and blogger at baringtheaegis.blogspot.com. She blogs daily about life in ancient Hellas, the theoi, and modern Hellenism with the goal of furthering understanding and practice of the ancient Hellenic religion.

Terence P. Ward realized he was Pagan after he bought his own copy of Drawing Down the Moon in 1988. His religious practices since have included being bound to a Wiccan coven, walking sacred trails as a backpacking Pagan or Gaiaped, raising energy with a number of loosely-organized collections of people, and being tapped by the Olympian gods. He is a polytheist with pantheistic and monistic sympathies, an animist approach to the world, and a respect for his ancestors. His personal practice includes daily offerings to Poseidon (whom he also serves as hiereus, temple priest) and weekly meeting for worship with his fellow Quakers.

Appendix D: About Bibliotheca Alexandrina

Ptolemy Soter, the first Makedonian ruler of Egypt, established the library at Alexandria to collect all of the world's learning in a single place. His scholars compiled definitive editions of the Classics, translated important foreign texts into Greek, and made monumental strides in science, mathematics, philosophy and literature. By some accounts over a million scrolls were housed in the famed library, and though it has long since perished due to the ravages of war, fire, and human ignorance, the image of this great institution has remained as a powerful inspiration down through the centuries.

To help promote the revival of traditional polytheistic religions we have launched a series of books dedicated to the ancient gods of Greece and Egypt. The library is a collaborative effort drawing on the combined resources of the different elements within the modern Hellenic and Kemetic communities, in the hope that we can come together to praise our gods and share our diverse understandings, experiences and approaches to the divine.

A list of our current and forthcoming titles can be found on the following page. For more information on the Bibliotheca, our submission requirements for upcoming devotionals, or to learn about our organization, please visit us at neosalexandria.org.

Sincerely,

The Editorial Board
of the Library of Neos Alexandria

Current Titles
Written in Wine: A Devotional Anthology for
    Dionysos
Dancing God: Poetry of Myths and Magicks
Goat Foot God
Longing for Wisdom: The Message of the Maxims
The Phillupic Hymns
Unbound: A Devotional Anthology for Artemis
Waters of Life: A Devotional Anthology for Isis and
    Serapis
Bearing Torches: A Devotional Anthology for
    Hekate
Queen of the Great Below: An Anthology in Honor
    of Ereshkigal
From Cave to Sky: A Devotional Anthology in
    Honor of Zeus
Out of Arcadia: A Devotional Anthology for Pan
Anointed: A Devotional Anthology for the Deities
    of the Near and Middle East
The Scribing Ibis: An Anthology of Pagan Fiction in
    Honor of Thoth

Queen of the Sacred Way: A Devotional Anthology in Honor of Persephone
Unto Herself: A Devotional Anthology for Independent Goddesses
The Shining Cities: An Anthology of Pagan Science Fiction
Guardian of the Road: A Devotional Anthology in Honor of Hermes
Harnessing Fire: A Devotional Anthology in Honor of Hephaestus
Beyond the Pillars: An Anthology of Pagan Fantasy
Queen of Olympos: A Devotional Anthology for Hera and Iuno
A Mantle of Stars: A Devotional Anthology in Honor of the Queen of Heaven
Crossing the River: An Anthology in Honor of Sacred Journeys
Ferryman of Souls: A Devotional for Charon
By Blood, Bone, and Blade: A Tribute to the Morrigan
Potnia: An Anthology in Honor of Demeter
The Queen of the Sky Who Rules Over All the Gods: A Devotional Anthology in Honor of Bast
From the Roaring Deep: A Devotional for Poseidon and the Spirits of the Sea
Daughter of the Sun: A Devotional Anthology in Honor of Sekhmet
Seasons of Grace: A Devotional in Honor of the Muses, the Charites, and the Horae

Lunessence: A Devotional for Selene
Les Cabinets des Polythéistes: An Anthology of Pagan Fairy Tales, Folktales, and Nursery Rhymes
With Lyre and Bow: A Devotional in Honor of Apollo
Garland of the Goddess: Tales and Poems of the Feminine Divine
The Dark Ones: Tales and Poems of the Shadow Gods
First and Last: A Devotional for Hestia

Forthcoming Titles
Dauntless: A Devotional in Honor of Ares and Mars
At the Gates of Dawn and Dusk: A Devotional for Eos and Aurora
The Far-Shining One: A Devotional for Helios and the Spirits of the Sun
Blood and Roses: A Devotional in Honor of Aphrodite and Venus
A Silver Sun and Inky Clouds: A Devotional for Djehuty and Set